Shown Approved

Shown Approved

Philadelphian Christianity and Jesus'
Letter to the Church

BY Cynthia C. Polsley

FOREWORD BY
Greg Ammons

WIPF & STOCK · Eugene, Oregon

SHOWN APPROVED
Philadelphian Christianity and Jesus' Letter to the Church

Copyright © 2024 Cynthia C. Polsley. All rights reserved. Except for brief quotations in critical publications or reviews, no part of this book may be reproduced in any manner without prior written permission from the publisher. Write: Permissions, Wipf and Stock Publishers, 199 W. 8th Ave., Suite 3, Eugene, OR 97401.

Wipf & Stock
An Imprint of Wipf and Stock Publishers
199 W. 8th Ave., Suite 3
Eugene, OR 97401

www.wipfandstock.com

PAPERBACK ISBN: 979-8-3852-2501-9
HARDCOVER ISBN: 979-8-3852-2502-6
EBOOK ISBN: 979-8-3852-2503-3

VERSION NUMBER 09/16/24

All direct quotations of Scripture are taken from the King James Version (KJV) and are in the public domain in the United States of America. Translations of ancient Greek and Latin secular texts are the author's unless otherwise noted.

Dedication

To the believers of the OCC Revelation Sunday School and Wednesday groups, in loving memory of those who have preceded us into the Lord Jesus' presence (Col 3:4); and to Mariam, Lee, and your three, knowing that the best is yet to come (Eph 1:4–5).

In all things, "To the only wise God our Saviour, be glory and majesty, dominion and power, both now and ever. Amen" (Jude 25).

Study to shew thyself approved unto God,
a workman that needeth not to be ashamed,
rightly dividing the word of truth.

—2 Tim 2:15

Contents

Foreword by Dr. Greg Ammons | ix
Acknowledgments | xii
Scripture Abbreviations | xiii
Prologue: The Road to Philadelphia | xv
Text of the Letter to the Church of Philadelphia (Rev 3:7–13) | xxi

1 Reading Revelation | 1
2 A Survey of the Seven Churches | 9
3 Holiness and Wholeness | 20
4 The Bedrock of Truth | 29
5 The King and His Keys | 38
6 Opportunity, an Open-and-Shut Case | 46
7 Weakness, Meekness, and Other Strengths | 54
8 Keeping the Word, Keeping the Faith | 62
9 In One Word, Salvation | 70
10 The Church as the Church | 80
11 Of Patience and Promises | 88
12 Jesus, Coming Quickly | 97
13 Imminency and the Christian's Action Plan | 105
14 Citizens of God's Country | 112

Epilogue: Continuing on the Philadelphian-Wannabe Journey | 123
Appendix A: How to Be Saved | 131
Appendix B: Historical Philadelphia | 135
Bibliography | 143
Subject Index | 145
Scripture Index | 151

Foreword

It stood shimmering six hundred and fifty feet above the sea. Behind it lay volcanic cliffs, the result of numerous earthquakes in the region. On one side of it was exceedingly fertile land, which grew numerous and luscious fruits. Through it was the Imperial Post Road, an important trade route of the first century. Yet the strength of the metropolis lay deep within the heart of the city, its people—not just any people group but specifically early believers in Jesus Christ.

I am speaking of the ancient city of Philadelphia. This sparkling city was founded after 189 BC on an ancient highway system leading to the interior of Asia Minor. A small group of believers in Jesus Christ formed in the city of Philadelphia soon after the resurrection and subsequent ascension of the Savior. It is possible that some of the three thousand believers at Pentecost were residents of the region around Philadelphia and brought the gospel to the region soon after.

As John began writing letters to the seven churches of Asia Minor, under the inspiration of the Holy Spirit in chapters 2 and 3 of Revelation, there was a special message for the believers in Philadelphia. The sixth of John's seven letters to these ancient churches, the letter to the believers at Philadelphia, was unique. It was only one of two churches for whom our Savior had no words of rebuke, only words of commendation.

In Rev 3:7-13, God affirmed the positive actions of the Philadelphian believers. "I know thy works. . . . I have set before thee an open door, and no man can shut it: for thou hast a little strength, and hast kept my word, and hast not denied my name" (Rev 3:8). Then, the Spirit condemned the enemies of the Philadelphian church and encouraged the early believers to stay faithful in persecution, knowing of future blessings that are theirs in heaven.

What did this small group of believers do differently than other churches who received harsh rebuke? How did they stay faithful to the Lord Jesus Christ during a time of persecution when the culture was against them? How do flourishing, faithful believers in Jesus today emulate the faith and actions of the Philadelphian church? How can we pursue a more meaningful, intentional Christian journey that pleases the Lord in a culture often antagonistic toward the Christian message?

Addressing these questions and more through a Scriptural lens, with reflection questions, action steps, and life lessons for application and growth, *Shown Approved* takes readers through Jesus' letter to the church in Philadelphia in Revelation.

My friend, Dr. Cara Polsley, has done a masterful job in putting together an academic and thorough, yet practical and applicable work that examines more closely the faith and actions of the early believers in Philadelphia. Dr. Polsley stated so wonderfully, "Philadelphia is a Christ-first, Christ-focused example for modern believers, offering encouragement and direction in the midst of an increasingly anti-biblical culture, promoting biblical literacy and awareness, and serving as a road map for healthy, humble, and mission-minded faith in action."[1]

Dr. Polsley is most qualified to write on the topic. She is a Bible scholar who teaches biblical exegesis, languages and civilization, and narratology. The author is also a classical philologist, researcher, and speaker. An alumna of the University of Kansas, Dr. Polsley also received her PhD in classics from Yale University. She has a strong faith in Jesus and a spirit of perseverance as a spinal cord injury survivor. She knows what it means to stay faithful in the midst of difficulty. She has authored a number of books, including *The Bible and the Holographic Universe*. I had the privilege of writing a recommendation for Dr. Polsley's book *A Primer on Messianic Prophecy*.

The author is masterful in taking you into the mind, setting, and culture of the Philadelphian church of the first century. From setting the historical stage to placing the writing in its cultural context to examining Jesus' commendations, the book delves into Philadelphian faith. Yet, like any efficacious writer, Dr. Polsley does not leave the reader in the first century. Her application is pertinent to contemporary readers, especially in chapter 8, "Keeping the Word, Keeping the Faith."

1. Cynthia C. Polsley, email message to author, Apr. 29, 2024.

FOREWORD

The work discusses the rapture and prophecy in a context that is meant to have believers thinking, not just about current events, but about being salt and light within the contemporary culture. It can be equally difficult for modern believers to live out their faith in the current culture, just as it was for the Philadelphian believers to live out their faith in the Laodicean culture. Fittingly, Dr. Polsley's work concludes with an appendix stating how to become a follower of Jesus.

My prayer is that you will encounter the same Spirit of God within the pages of this book who worked in and through the believers in Philadelphia in the first century. May the Father only have commendation for you as you seek to keep his command to endure patiently. May the Father know your deeds and place before you an open door of blessing that no one can shut.

Dr. Greg Ammons, Senior Pastor

First Baptist Church, Garland, Texas

Acknowledgments

As with all other works, this book would not be possible without special individuals who have offered support, whether they knew it or not. I am grateful to the quiet beta readers who acted behind the scenes and read drafts of the various chapters, as well as to the members of numerous study groups for working through the material. I would especially like to thank Dr. Greg Ammons for writing the foreword to this book. His friendship and faithful service for the Lord are an inspiration. Thank you to my family and friends for their continuous encouragement and love, particularly to my imaginative nieces and nephews (yes, still the best). May they all be true Philadelphian Christians at heart.

Scripture Abbreviations

Old Testament

Gen	Genesis	Eccl	Ecclesiastes
Exod	Exodus	Song	Song of Solomon
Lev	Leviticus	Isa	Isaiah
Num	Numbers	Jer	Jeremiah
Deut	Deuteronomy	Lam	Lamentations
Josh	Joshua	Ezek	Ezekiel
Judg	Judges	Dan	Daniel
Ruth	Ruth	Hos	Hosea
1 Sam	1 Samuel	Joel	Joel
2 Sam	2 Samuel	Amos	Amos
1 Kgs	1 Kings	Obad	Obadiah
2 Kgs	2 Kings	Jonah	Jonah
1 Chr	1 Chronicles	Mic	Micah
2 Chr	2 Chronicles	Nah	Nahum
Ezra	Ezra	Hab	Habakkuk
Neh	Nehemiah	Zeph	Zephaniah
Esth	Esther	Hag	Haggai
Job	Job	Zech	Zechariah
Ps	Psalms	Mal	Malachi
Prov	Proverbs		

SCRIPTURE ABBREVIATIONS

New Testament

Matt	Matthew	1 Tim	1 Timothy
Mark	Mark	2 Tim	2 Timothy
Luke	Luke	Titus	Titus
John	John	Phlm	Philemon
Acts	Acts	Heb	Hebrews
Rom	Romans	Jas	James
1 Cor	1 Corinthians	1 Pet	1 Peter
2 Cor	2 Corinthians	2 Pet	2 Peter
Gal	Galatians	1 John	1 John
Eph	Ephesians	2 John	2 John
Phil	Philippians	3 John	3 John
Col	Colossians	Jude	Jude
1 Thess	1 Thessalonians	Rev	Revelation
2 Thess	2 Thessalonians		

Prologue

The Road to Philadelphia

The topic of this book is Philadelphian Christianity, but what is Philadelphian Christianity in the first place? Surely it's not about the modern city of Philadelphia, Pennsylvania, is it? No, we're not talking about Christians living in Pennsylvania, although Christians do live there; and no, Philadelphian Christianity is not about Christians with special connections to the American city's sports teams or East Coast culture. Philadelphian Christianity doesn't involve serving Philly cheesesteaks for communion or sounding the Liberty Bell at the opening of every church service. It's something else altogether, in fact, something that's entirely, radically different. This is a something that, if we took it to heart, has the potential to transform our everyday walks with Jesus, both as individual Christians and as groups in Christ.

We have to go much further afield from twenty-first-century North America to discuss Philadelphian Christians, much less to become them. The process requires a transfer of space and time. Most of us have to shift continents completely. All of us have to think in terms of another century!

To talk about Philadelphian Christianity, we have to step back in time to the ancient city of Philadelphia. This Philadelphia, unlike the modern city of Philadelphia, Pennsylvania, was located in Asia Minor, modern Turkey. Ancient Philadelphia was founded by a pair of royal brothers in the second century BC. The first brother was Eumenes II, king of Pergamon, a.k.a. Pergamos/Pergamum. The second brother was Eumenes's successor, Attalus II. These brothers were so bonded that the city received its name in honor of their emotional attachment to each other. Philadelphia means "brotherly love." Attalus's nickname was Philadelphus, an epithet signaling the pair's brotherly affection for each other. For all else that they did and were, Eumenes II and Attalus II are today known mainly through the existence of the city named for their fraternal love. (For more on historical Philadelphia and the city's background, see appendix B.)

Philadelphian is a fitting name for the Christians we ought to be and for the brotherly love we should be known for sharing with each other. Of course, we are supposed to abound in our love for one another. Yet that love in itself is still not the primary source for what it means to be a Philadelphian Christian, nor is it why the term holds any significance for us today.

Our source for Philadelphian Christianity and its qualities is the Bible, which contains a description that comes straight from the mouth of Jesus Christ.

Rewinding to the ancient Philadelphia—the one that was founded by these two kingly brothers in the second century BC, almost two hundred years before Jesus' birth—we find that this city has a very important place in Scripture. Actually, it has an important role in Revelation, the very last book of the Bible.

Revelation 2 and 3 contain a series of seven letters dictated by the Lord Jesus to the apostle John at the end of the first century AD. The letters are addressed to seven particular churches in ancient Asia Minor. Philadelphia is one of these seven churches. Even more meaningfully, it is one of only two churches—just two!—that receive a total commendation. *Jesus has nothing bad to say about the church of Philadelphia.*

To put that in perspective, consider the seven churches as a whole in the book of Revelation. The seven are Ephesus, Smyrna, Pergamon, Thyatira, Sardis, Philadelphia, and Laodicea. Jesus speaks directly to each of these churches. Each one is located in a prominent city in the area of modern western Turkey. In addressing the cities, Jesus quickly establishes a pattern. He identifies himself by a specific title or set of titles, giving qualities of his character. He then commends the church that is receiving the letter, listing positive points that the certain church has or noting that he has seen their efforts to serve him. With most of the churches, the positive list is immediately followed by a strong contrast: "I know that you've done that good thing, *but* . . ."

What follows is a condemnation or a criticism of the church's conduct or attitude. Jesus is not being unduly harsh. He is being righteous and holy. There are serious issues in these churches, and if they don't deal with these problems, the people are going to lose their intimacy with him. Their situation is due to the state of their heart as a unit. Jesus offers a heart transplant that is sorely needed.

Fortunately, the condemnation is typically accompanied by a word of direction. The churches may be on course to their self-destruction, but they don't have to be. If they'll listen to Christ's admonition, they still have time to recover. Even though they may have lost their way, here is Jesus, "the way" (John 14:6), showing them how to find him. Jesus wants them to turn to him and to be strong until the end. He never leaves them or us without a way forward. He is the Way, if only we are willing to submit ourselves and be obedient.

Finally, after Jesus' evaluation of each church, the pattern of the letters in Revelation carries a promise for overcomers. If they turn to Jesus and hold fast to him, faithful Christians can expect to receive a wonderful reward. Every church receives the promise, because the opportunity is available to individuals. The church of each city is an institution. It is the individuals inside the church institution whom Jesus is addressing. He wants hearts, not rituals or buildings. That is why all of the letters contain the same phrase: "He that hath an ear, let him hear what the Spirit saith unto the churches" (Rev 2:7a). Jesus is not speaking only to those with physical ears. He is addressing anybody with any spiritual hearing. Anyone and everyone should be listening to what he has to say.

Jesus' reference to spiritual hearing means that these letters are not merely for first-century Christians in these seven cities of ancient Asia Minor. They are also recorded for us. As we've seen, they are part of the book of Revelation, and that is particularly significant because the book of Revelation is the only book in the Bible to guarantee a special blessing for those who dwell on it: "Blessed is he that readeth, and they that hear the words of this prophecy, and keep those things which are written therein: for the time is at hand" (Rev 1:3).

Jesus wants everyone to be reading these letters. Whether or not you are a Christian, he wants you to read these letters.

That being said, even though these letters are written for all to hear and read, the letters have a decidedly different meaning for Christians than they do for non-Christians. No one but Christians can have an intimate relationship with Jesus Christ; Christianity is all about an intimate relationship with Jesus Christ. Eternal life is found in knowing the God of the Bible as the only true God, and in knowing Jesus Christ, whom he has sent and who is one with the Father (John 17:3, 10:30). For non-Christians, reading these letters should be a step toward finding true life in Jesus Christ. You cannot be saved through doing good works or joining a church. You can be saved if you turn to the One who sent these messages.

For those who have been saved and are already Christians, what is the point of reading these letters? What do we gain from Rev 2–3? One benefit of these chapters and the letters they contain is that they are sent to help us keep ourselves in line with the will of God. To serve the Lord properly, we must always be examining our own hearts. We must always be seeking a stronger relationship with him and striving to know him more fully. To achieve those goals, we must know what he cares about, and we must let him transform us so that we, too, come to care about the same things. Jesus cared enough to take the time to compose these letters. Their contents and recipients clearly matter to him. If they matter to our Lord, they ought to matter just as much to us.

This leads us to a second benefit of the seven letters: reading them should evoke self-examination. Jesus is essentially "grading" these churches. He is showing them how he sees them, not how they see themselves or how the world views them. The evaluation process in these chapters centers on what Christ sees when his perfect, holy eyes look at these groups. These letters reveal the true states of these churches' hearts. Going behind the scenes, or rather, going far above the stage for a truly comprehensive view, the letters reveal what God approves and disapproves of in these church institutions. What does he like? What does he not like? God's likes and dislikes are connected to his character, which is, in turn, intrinsically linked with what is healthy or unhealthy for the church. These letters and these churches are messages to us about what God desires to see in us. The letters capture pictures of morality and behavior.

There, then, is another vital benefit to paying attention and reading the letters in Rev 2–3. If these letters make us stop and consider what and who we are inside, and if they show us what God approves or disapproves of, then they show us what a healthy church looks like. They also show us what an unhealthy church looks like. What better place to start becoming stronger, livelier Christians than to study the churches that Jesus says are doing a good job? What are they doing right? How can we do what's right? How can we become Christians who both delight God and find delight in him, doing his will, honoring, and serving him?

That is the short description of faithful Christians practicing their faith, trying to live out their love for and commitment to Christ. They are Christians that bring him pleasure. They are, in biblical terms, Philadelphian Christians. The name "Philadelphian Christian" has its origins here in the letter to the church of Philadelphia in Rev 3. When Jesus grades the people of the Philadelphian church, the report is completely positive. These Christians are trying their best, focusing on him, and doing well. They need to keep striving to follow Jesus as they are now. Remembering what God has said and done, they have a special future and a special promise all their own.

And that, in a nutshell, is the Lord's message to the church of Philadelphia.

But there's still much more to say about it, because this letter has much more to it than that. Jesus' words tell us about holiness, truth, purpose, love, and more. His message is far more specific than it might appear. His words are well suited to the Philadelphians in their historical, immediate context, as well as to us in ours today. In the midst of a confused world that seeks to redefine the Church, Christianity, and Jesus himself, it is high time to reclaim Philadelphian Christianity. Our actions and reactions need to be proactively, purposefully based on Christ and our place in him.

The decisions we make about serving Jesus are not being made in a vacuum. Increasingly, the world is tugging, pulling, yanking on each and every heart. Society is forcing hard choices that are always already in play in the broader scheme of spiritual warfare. In response to muddied priorities, watered-down doctrines, confusing claims, satanic attacks on Scripture, and generally deceptive assaults on every aspect of life, and in the face of unfolding prophecies, global fears, and unmatched cultural shifts, what can we do? For Christians, the solution is found at the core of what we say we believe. We must go back to Jesus Christ for our peace and hope, and we must return to him as the source of truth. Now is the time to embrace our identity in Jesus alone and to seek a healthier faith in him.

What qualities, though, does Jesus want in a church? In individuals? What are the qualities of this Philadelphian church that is so pleasing to him? Not intrinsic perfection. God does not expect believers to be perfect on our own, or else there would not be a gospel. If we were not inherently sinful, there would be no need for Jesus to bring salvation. The truth of the gospel is that, left to ourselves, we are all imperfect sinners doomed to hell due to our own actions, thoughts, and behaviors. As we'll see, the

Philadelphian mindset highlights the truth of the gospel by concentrating on Jesus' inherent perfection and holiness. Philadelphian Christianity keeps its eyes fixed on the Savior. It is practical and intentional. It is not a subset of Christianity. There are no identity groups within Christ's true Body, the Church. Heaven does not have denominational sections for Philadelphian Christians on one side and Smyrnan Christians on the other, for instance. Yet the term "Philadelphian Christianity" can be helpful for us, because it expresses the traits of faithful, fruitful Christianity in action. We are viewing an approved church and its attributes through the lens of Christ's own words.

The world is wandering and lost in its own sins, but the Church as the Body of Jesus is meant to be his and to find significance in him. *The time is now.* We desperately need a healthy infusion of Philadelphian Christianity today. But we still come back to the same major concerns: What makes a Philadelphian Christian? What makes a church or an individual the recipient of Jesus' direct approval? In a confused world of spiritualism, apathy, and apostasy, what is our response? What does God want us to be doing, and how can we do it?

Those questions are the topic of this book. They are ever pertinent in a darkening world that needs the light of Jesus more than ever. These are questions that can change the direction of a life and alter the course of a family or a church. They can have a ripple effect of revival. If the cry of your heart is to find answers to these questions and others like them, and if you want to pursue a more meaningful relationship with Jesus Christ, know that Jesus is listening. He is speaking. He's already had a lot to say about the heart that pleases him!

I don't know about you, but I want to be a Philadelphian Christian. I'm an unashamed Philadelphian-wannabe. If that description fits you, too, then turn to Rev 3, and let's get started on the path.

Text of the Letter to the Church of Philadelphia (Rev 3:7–13)

And to the angel of the church in Philadelphia write; These things saith he that is holy, he that is true, he that hath the key of David, he that openeth, and no man shutteth; and shutteth, and no man openeth; I know thy works: behold, I have set before thee an open door, and no man can shut it: for thou hast a little strength, and hast kept my word, and hast not denied my name. Behold, I will make them of the synagogue of Satan, which say they are Jews, and are not, but do lie; behold, I will make them to come and worship before thy feet, and to know that I have loved thee. Because thou hast kept the word of my patience, I also will keep thee from the hour of temptation, which shall come upon all the world, to try them that dwell upon the earth. Behold, I come quickly: hold that fast which thou hast, that no man take thy crown. Him that overcometh will I make a pillar in the temple of my God, and he shall go no more out: and I will write upon him the name of my God, and the name of the city of my God, which is new Jerusalem, which cometh down out of heaven from my God: and I will write upon him my new name. He that hath an ear, let him hear what the Spirit saith unto the churches.

1

Reading Revelation

> Blessed is he that readeth, and they that hear the words of this prophecy, and keep those things which are written therein: for the time is at hand. —Rev 1:3

To BETTER UNDERSTAND THE Philadelphians, let's consider more deeply the biblical context of Jesus' letter to them. The letter to Philadelphia is second to last in a series of seven letters. While the letters are directly addressed to the seven churches named by Jesus, we know that they are intended to be read by anyone who will pay attention. Revelation declares that the letters are for us. Not only does the book's opening confer an unparalleled blessing upon all of those who listen to it, read it aloud, and keep its words (Rev 1:3), but Jesus repeats a strong admonition throughout chapters 2 through 3 of Revelation. "He that hath an ear, let him hear what the Spirit saith unto the churches" (Rev 2:7a, 11a, 17a, 29; 3:6, 13, 22). Every single letter contains this same declaration. Christ is issuing an invitation as well as a forceful warning. These letters are designed to be a testimony, correction, and instruction for all of us.

Reading between the lines, these letters are packed with tailor-made insights and nuances that contemporary readers easily overlook. Jesus chooses certain titles for himself when he addresses the churches. He selects churches bearing names that resemble their respective character traits. On the surface alone, these are seven actual churches in Asia Minor. We know that each one of them really did exist, and that the smallest details of the letters have special meaning for these specific locations and cities. Jesus was not being poetic or appealing to the imagination. John knew the churches and the cities being discussed. He would have recognized many of the key elements in the letters. Additionally, he knew where and how to "post" these letters so that the mail could reach its intended destination! In the ancient world, these cities were big names. Being famous and boasting famous associations with premium trade guilds, historical events, and unique situations, the cities' names would have conveyed more information to any first-century Roman reader than to us today. It seems obvious enough that original readers would have comprehended more of the letters' relevance to them personally, but we miss just how much intention is latent in every phrase.

That being said, we already know that these letters are intended for everyone. "He that hath an ear, let him hear what the Spirit saith unto the churches" (Rev 3:13). These churches are models. They are not all role models, but they are models in that they are "types." For one thing, they are types for us as individuals. Christians should be examining ourselves in the light of what Jesus says about these churches. As archetypes, the churches are guides for us to measure ourselves against as we read and listen to the letters. Remember, we are not trying to measure up to any churches or to the people in them. We are reading what Jesus says and applying his words to our personal relationships with him. This individual level of reading affects how we live out our faith.

Another level of impact exists for church institutions today. The letters' recipients were seven real-life churches with real-life meeting spaces and worship times. They met in physical buildings. They read Scripture. They sang and took communion together. Broadly speaking, though metaphorically worlds and years apart from us, they are not that unlike our churches in the twenty-first century. How close are their attitudes and customs to ours? Are we practicing the same good habits they have? Or, on the flip side, are we exhibiting the same bad qualities they have? Do our priorities match theirs, and should they? Whatever Jesus said to these churches is a standard for us to observe. The letters are letters to us as communities of Christians. They are letters written for church institutions and their leadership, congregations, small groups, Sunday Schools, boards, and ministries.

Even more broadly, another level of meaning emerges as we read the seven letters in order. These seven churches reflect the development of the church institution as a whole across the generations. Ephesus (church #1) is called a church that began in fellowship with the Lord, but has lost its first love. Ephesus fits the description of an apostolic church full of people who walked and talked with Jesus first-hand. These eyewitnesses initially experience close fellowship with him. Their love for him forms around that fellowship and close-knit bond. Ephesus readily corresponds to the historical early church. The early church was built on the foundation of the testimony of eyewitnesses who had fellowship with Jesus during his time on the earth. Those who did not physically meet Jesus himself were acquainted with the apostles who had literally walked beside him.

Soon after its birth, the early church developed into a large number of church institutions, many full of Christians suffering persecution from the Roman authorities and others. The persecuted church that grew out of the early church is equivalent to Smyrna, the second church in Rev 2. Jesus' letter to the suffering church of Smyrna (church #2) equates to an age of intense persecution that was inflicted on believers in the mid to late first century and following years.

One thing led to another, and many people in the churches began to compromise with the world. Their state of compromise is mirrored in Pergamon (Pergamos), the third church of Revelation. Pergamon (#3) aptly reflects the fourth-century marriage of the established church and the secular world under Emperor Constantine. After Pergamon, we can trace a clear route to worse corruption, as seen in Thyatira (#4) and the ritualistic, organized church system of the Dark and Middle Ages.

Revelation's tour of the churches continues to parallel with the historical march of the church institution overall. The corrupt church of Thyatira eventually collapses into a dead church, visible in Revelation's church of Sardis (#5). A revival after the Reformation leads to an explosion in Protestant missionary movements in the early twentieth century. The mission-minded church of impactful evangelism is equivalent to Philadelphia (#6). And, unfortunately, the last-days church has its greatest internal struggle (and even demise) in the throes of apostasy, evident in the life of a church that believes it is more aware than ever but is utterly blind, wretched, and lost. This fallen, nominal church, called Laodicea (#7), will be more prominent than ever as history reaches its climax. Chronologically, moving through the seven churches, we pass through the life of the church institution from the early church stretching all the way to an apostate, in-name-only church.

We should note a few critical points about this chronological look at the life of the church as an institution. These insights from Revelation help us to remember that Christ will always have his Church, in spite of the world's best—and, yes, worst!—efforts to destroy it. Most importantly, there is a distinct difference between what we call the Church Invisible (the Body of Christ) and Church Visible (the church institution). A real Body of believers, the real Church, will always exist, even though God alone possesses the real membership roster. The Church of Christ is described in 1 Cor 12:

> For as the body is one, and hath many members, and all the members of that one body, being many, are one body: so also is Christ. For by one Spirit are we all baptized into one body, whether we be Jews or Gentiles, whether we be bond or free; and have been all made to drink into one Spirit. (vv. 12–13)

Ever since the advent of the Holy Spirit upon Christians in Acts 2, the Church has been Christ's Body on earth. Ephesians explains, "There is one body, and one Spirit, even as ye are called in one hope of your calling" (4:4). Every Christian alive today is a member of the Church.

The Bible further reveals that the Church is Christ's Bride. In Eph 5, Paul speaks of the relationship between a husband and wife. He describes the depth of love and sacrifice involved in a healthy marriage. In a pivotal passage, Paul writes that husbands should love their wives "as Christ also loved the church, and gave himself for it" (v. 25b). He adds,

> For no man ever yet hated his own flesh; but nourisheth and cherisheth it, even as the Lord the church: For we are members of his body, of his flesh, and of his bones. For this cause shall a man leave his father and mother, and shall be joined unto his wife, and they two shall be one flesh. This is a great mystery: but I speak concerning Christ and the church. (vv. 29–32)

The mystery of Christ and the Church refers to the loving relationship between Jesus and believers, those who have entrusted Jesus with their souls and come to him for cleansing from sins. No one can become part of Christ's Body by any other means. His Body, the Church, is the Church Invisible. The Church Invisible is not a building, organization, or institution.

Meanwhile, the church institution, or Church Visible, is not the same as the Body of Christ, the Church Invisible. Many Christians attend church institutions and are part of the Church Visible. These believers are members of the Church Invisible (a.k.a., the Body, Christ's Bride) as well as the Church Visible (the institution). Other people can be in the opposite situation. They may attend the Church Visible and be prominent members in a church congregation without ever choosing to enter into a personal relationship with Jesus Christ. Therefore, being unbelievers, they never become part of the Church Invisible, even though they belong to the Church Visible. Only the state of your heart and your relationship with Jesus Christ determine your membership in the Church Invisible. Jesus "is the head of the body, the church" (Col 1:18).

As for the historical development of the Church Visible in Rev 2–3, different types of institutional churches can coexist across time. In the stages represented in the Revelation churches, we observe a shift from a more interpersonal early church to an apostate anti-church. No type of church institution is necessarily exclusive for its own period in history. There is no age in which there are not some apostate churches or some martyr churches, for instance. The Church Invisible is always engaging in a battle with bad doctrine and invasive teachings, which inevitably find their way into the various church institutions of the Church Visible.

In sum, the view of the seven churches as a time line of church development does not imply that there is a strict chronology and that the church goes from type 1 to type 2 to type 3, and so forth. The general development of the church institution displays a basic series of changes over time. At different times, one kind of church institution or cultural shift may be more or less visible on the world stage. Such are the changes and trends observed in Rev 2–3.

Types of churches continue across time. They do not end because a century closes or because an empire fades away. Faithful churches existed in the first century; Philadelphia did, and it was a missionary church. Faithful churches still do exist today. By the same token, faithless churches existed in the first century, too. Laodicea did. It was a real-life church institution with real-life apostasy. It was a nominal church, and there it was, existing in the first century. What we see in Revelation is a linear pattern of church development. The manner in which the church changes draws attention to the prevailing spirit of an age, as revealed in the state of the church at the time. These ages and trends show the general direction of cultures and civilizations. They are not mutually exclusive, although sometimes cultures and churches sway one way more than another.

Mainly, the development of the church across time reflects a march toward the world's final decision to rebel against God. This worldly rebellion is detailed in Revelation and elsewhere in Scripture. Often, church development contributes to pushing history along in its course. When the church is a corrupt and weak institution, and when the Church Invisible is overshadowed by a more active, less moral Church Visible, society tends to take massive leaps in the wrong direction.

Again, none of these readings (historical, individual, collective, or chronological) cancel each other out. We have explored four levels of the application of these letters: *historically*, how they show real-life historical churches in Asia Minor; *individually* and *collectively*, how they work as evaluations that we can use for ourselves as individuals in growing closer to Jesus and as groups in church communities; and *chronologically*, how they reflect the church institution's changes over time. All four levels have significance and importance. All four levels should bring us back to the truth of who Jesus is and how we deal with that truth. Just because we focus on one level does not mean that we are denying the legitimacy of another.

The key to any biblical interpretation, however, holds true here as with any other method of close reading in Scripture. We must read the Bible's content in its own context. How does the Bible interpret itself for us? "No prophecy of the scripture is of any private interpretation," Peter reminds us in 2 Pet 1:20b. He's not telling believers to quit reading Scripture privately or to think that we cannot understand it. He's affirming that God is communicating absolute, unchanging truths. When we try to reinterpret the Bible and make it fit our own mold, we're fighting against that truth.

If we are reading the Bible honestly as it presents itself, we have to let it do the interpretation in its own context. We have to throw away our own mold for what the Bible should say and what we should be. As Christians, we have to let God shape our principles and ideals. "For the prophecy came not in the old time by the will of man: but holy men of God spake as they were moved by the Holy Ghost" (2 Pet 1:21). The phrase "as they were moved by the Holy Ghost" is essential. It indicates that every single detail in prophecy originates from the Holy Spirit. God inspires his Word. He breathes his breath into it, decides every single letter, and determines every detail of every message. We *should* read the Bible privately and collectively. But whenever we read or listen to it, we should not be trying to change it, but rather to let it change us. Scripture has its own context, just as it has its own content. The Bible needs to become our context and our content, as well. It needs to become our framework, determine our worldview, and guide every aspect of what and who we are. The more we align with Jesus, the more we will be changed from the inside out.

The holy inspiration of the Bible as the Word of God cannot be overestimated. Through the Holy Bible, we learn more and more about God. Consequently, we see more and more how he never changes and is always true. The Bible demonstrates his truth and faithfulness. Its contents are so intricate and detailed that every single aspect of it matters. In Matt 5, refuting allegations that he was trying to demolish the Mosaic law, Jesus made a statement that stands the test of the ages. "For verily I say unto you, Till heaven and earth pass, one jot or one tittle shall in no wise pass from the law, till all be fulfilled" (v. 18). Jots and tittles are the smallest letters and marks in the Hebrew alphabet and its writing. God organized his book so that even these jots and tittles have the greatest importance. We have to acknowledge his divine authorship and admit that the Bible is written by his design. We must let it be his book and let him tell us what he means to communicate. God's authorship is visible on every level of Scripture, no matter how big or small it appears to us.

Operating on these principles, how are we to approach the seven letters? The answer has to come from the same source. Each one of us should come to the seven church letters with an open heart and open mind, allowing God to move as he will, and allowing the Bible to interpret itself for us. The book of Revelation, just like the rest of Scripture, is the inspired Word of God. As Christians, if we take it as it is given and admit that the Bible is God's inspired and inerrant Word, then we must treat Revelation as a sacred communication from the Lord to us as individuals and groups. Second Timothy declares,

> All scripture is given by inspiration of God, and is profitable for doctrine, for reproof, for correction, for instruction in righteousness: That the man of God may be perfect, thoroughly furnished unto all good works. (3:16–17)

The book of Revelation is included in the Bible. Like all other Scripture, it is meant to teach, instruct, direct, correct, and train us. If we neglect Revelation, we're ignoring a vital part of our training course, exercise program, core curriculum. Historically, chronologically, jointly, and personally, these letters in Rev 2–3 are written for us. We ought to learn from them and seek to grow in Christ through them. Everything in them is about Jesus and our relationship with him.

As if that were not enough, it's again worth remembering that Revelation carries a special blessing for those who read it and take it to heart. The very beginning of Rev 1 contains a blessing that is echoed nowhere else in

Scripture: "Blessed is he that readeth, and they that hear the words of this prophecy, and keep those things which are written therein: for the time is at hand" (v. 3). The seven letters to the seven churches are not excluded from this blessing. They are part of Revelation. They are so important that they set the tone for what follows. In reading and studying them, we are acting in obedience. From reading and studying them, we grow in that obedience. And in reflecting on them repeatedly, approaching them as we do the rest of the Bible, we find that we never finish scratching the surface of their significance for us on every single level of life.

2

A Survey of the Seven Churches

> What thou seest, write in a book, and send it unto the seven churches which are in Asia; unto Ephesus, and unto Smyrna, and unto Pergamos, and unto Thyatira, and unto Sardis, and unto Philadelphia, and unto Laodicea. —Rev 1:11b

IF EVERY ELEMENT OF the letters in Rev 2–3 is packed with significance from beginning to end, a short survey of the other churches will only help to put Philadelphia in greater context. But readers should be advised: These letters are designed for you, and there's a lot more to discover in reading them than in reading a short introduction! Don't let this book and its overview of the chapters stand in for your own reading of Rev 2–3. Read for yourself, read again, and don't stop reading. Read aloud, read silently, read early, read late, and read often.

Ephesus is the first church in the series of letters. In addressing Ephesus, Jesus calls himself the One "that holdeth the seven stars in his right hand, who walketh in the midst of the seven golden candlesticks" (Rev 2:1b). These attributes look back to Rev 1 and speak of the fellowship that Jesus has with his church. They also look ahead to the substance of the letter to Ephesus. This is going to be a letter all about fellowship—fellowship once possessed, then lost, and to be regained by anyone who will pay attention. Christians who heed the warnings of this letter can expect a unique reward of fellowship and entry into God's intimate presence. The name Ephesus means "desired one." In this letter, Jesus does indeed show his desire for hearts. His Church is his desired one.

From the outset, the Ephesians are commended for their deeds, hard work, and patience. These people have a particularly good habit of testing what teachers tell them. "Thou hast tried them which say they are apostles, and are not, and hast found them liars," Jesus says (Rev 2:2b). Believers at Ephesus are uncompromising when it comes to evil. Christ applauds their refusal to tolerate bad doctrine in the church.

Nevertheless, as good as Ephesus looks on paper, it has a serious problem. Jesus has something major against them: "Thou hast left thy first love" (Rev 2:4b). He advises the Ephesians to remember where they once were, repent, and do what they used to do. If they do not repent, they will be removed from their place before Jesus (Rev 2:5). Here's the call to action for anyone who is listening and willing to follow through with Jesus' instructions: repent and return to fellowship with him.

Besides their wariness of treacherous doctrine and their refusal to compromise on morality, there are other good things about Ephesus. The Ephesians hate hierarchies and cult systems that come between individual believers and God (Rev 2:6). The churchgoers of Ephesus diligently work to remove anything that gets in the way of truth. Their conscientiousness affords them positive feedback from Jesus, who then offers another encouragement for the Ephesian overcomer. The faithful Christians of this church can expect to have a specific, wonderful fellowship with him: "To him that overcometh will I give to eat of the tree of life, which is in the midst of the paradise of God" (Rev 2:7b).

Jesus' special promise to the overcomers from Ephesus recalls what was lost due to human sin. At the beginning of time, before the first sin in the garden of Eden, the first humans Adam and Eve enjoyed a special fellowship in God's presence. Those faithful to pursue Jesus and to be his desired one have the promise of enjoying such intimacy again someday. We can read all about it in Rev 21 and 22, with the joys of the new heaven and new earth.

The second church in the Revelation letters' line-up is Smyrna. Jesus identifies himself to Smyrna as the first and the last, who was dead and is now alive. "I know thy works, and tribulation, and poverty, (but thou art rich) and I know the blasphemy of them which say they are Jews, and are not, but are the synagogue of Satan" (Rev 2:9). The Christians of Smyrna are suffering, impoverished Christians. They are struggling under the weight of intense persecution from both gentiles and Jews. The persecution was not unexpected. Before his crucifixion and resurrection, the Lord had told the

Jewish believers to expect hatred from other Jews who denied him. "They shall put you out of the synagogues: yea, the time cometh, that whosoever killeth you will think that he doeth God service" (John 16:2).

Smyrna's name reflects its situation. The name Smyrna is related to the precious gum-resin myrrh. Myrrh is harvested through a process of crushing and bruising the tree. Similarly, the precious Christians of Smyrna are being wounded, bruised, and crushed. Their suffering is creating a testimony that honors God. Since they are growing closer to him and bearing a good witness, they are even more approved of and honored in his sight. "Precious in the sight of the Lord is the death of his saints" (Ps 116:15). Just as the precious, expensive substance of myrrh results from a procedure of crushing and bruising, so too does the crushing of the Smyrnans result in a fragrant, precious sacrifice to God. As the afflicted apostle Paul puts it, "For we are unto God a sweet savour of Christ" (2 Cor 2:15a).

Jesus expresses no disfavor toward the church of Smyrna. These Christians are going through enough already. They will later be rewarded, but they have more adversity to face in the meantime. Some will be thrown into prison. Some will die. "Be thou faithful unto death, and I will give thee a crown of life" (Rev 2:10b). The second death of hell has no claim on the faithful overcomers of Smyrna. Even though they may die now, they will live forever.

Smyrna receives hard news in the report that more persecution is to come, but they have a great commendation from the Lord. Even so, the hard message to Smyrna is not as alarming as Jesus' words to the next church, Pergamon (Pergamos). Pergamon is built in the very heart of cultic activity. The city is home to the Pergamon Altar, a massive second-century BC structure dedicated to false gods. This city, Jesus says, is "where Satan's seat is" and "where Satan dwelleth" (Rev 2:13a, c). Pergamon is a church that needs discernment and must be very careful not to compromise in the face of so much evil. They need to be spiritually sharp and aware. Thus, in his address to them, Jesus calls himself the One who has "the sharp sword with two edges" (Rev 2:12b). His two-edged sword judges between true and false and good and evil. The church institution at Pergamon needs the sword of his Spirit to distinguish between the truth of Christ and the lies of the world.

In sore need of God's discernment, the heart of Pergamon instead reflects the meaning of the city's name. "Pergamon" means "a thorough marriage." These churchgoers are thoroughly mixed in a union with the world.

True, they have some faithful believers who are holding fast. Jesus refers to the example of Antipas, one of the noble martyrs slain at Pergamon (Rev 2:13b). The mention of the beloved martyr Antipas is a strong commendation for Pergamon, especially in such a dark place and time, weighed down by the presence of Satan and multitudes of demons. We do not know anything about the man Antipas except for his legacy through this letter. Yet what we do learn is enough. Jesus knows Antipas. This man's sacrifice was precious in God's sight. Antipas boasts a rich inheritance through Christ.

Still, Pergamon has some big issues, putting it mildly. "Thou has there them that hold the doctrine of Balaam" (Rev 2:14a). Balaam was the Mesopotamian prophet hired by the enemies of Israel in Num 22–24. Israel's foes paid him to curse the Jews. Instead, Balaam was led by God to bless the Jews.

Sadly, Balaam did not internalize the blessing on the Jews. He never blessed them wholeheartedly or willingly, and within the limits God allowed, Balaam chose to harm Israel as much as possible. Although he had been used to deliver a blessing and to prophesy about the Jews' bright future, Balaam went the other direction personally. He deliberately helped Israel's enemies to devise a plan to invade and destroy the Jewish people. The plan was simple enough. Balaam encouraged the enemy nations to intermarry with the Israelites. He taught Balak, the king of Moab, "to cast a stumblingblock before the children of Israel, to eat things sacrificed unto idols, and to commit fornication" (Rev 2:14b). By urging Moab and the other surrounding nations to ally with Israel through marriage, Balaam contributed to a deadly dangerous spiritual rot among the Jewish people.

Balaam's actions were not the only factor in the Jews' later idolatry, but they were a catalyst. Many Israelites failed to exercise their own discernment and fell prey to the trap. They actively became involved with the nearby pagan cultures and their neighbors' idol worship. All of this caused the incident of Baal Peor—the Jews' act of intermarrying with the world, directly going against God's law (Num 25:1–3; 31:16; Deut 4:3). The events of Baal Peor culminated in destruction, plague, and ongoing shame (Hos 9:10, Ps 106:28, 1 Cor 10:8).

Baal Peor became a byword for blending in with worldly desires. The bare mention of Balaam should distress the church institution at Pergamon. Pergamon, the city of "mixed marriage," can expect a similar outcome of judgment as a result of its intermarrying with the world. Like the ancient Jews at Baal Peor, Pergamon will face condemnation, if it does not exercise the discernment of the sword of the Spirit. The people need to be applying the Word in their everyday lives (Heb 4:12, Eph 6:17). Whereas Pergamon could learn a positive lesson from Ephesus when it comes to examining teaching and doctrine, instead the churchgoers at Pergamon uphold evil doctrines of priestcraft, human hierarchies, and ritual systems that come between people and God (Rev 2:15). "Repent!" Christ orders. If they don't, the people of Pergamon can expect that he'll apply the sword of his mouth against them (Rev 2:16). Jesus is merciful, but in his mercy, he will not forever tolerate unrighteousness.

For those who listen and hear the Lord's commands, Jesus gives another promise to the true Church within the church institution at Pergamon. Overcomers in this church will receive the bread of life (hidden manna) and an inscribed stone denoting their relationship to the Lord (Rev 2:17). The stone represents access. It's also a reminder of the exclusivity of truth. We must all choose between Jesus and the world. We cannot have both.

As badly off as Pergamon is, the next church, Thyatira, is in just as dire or even worse straits. Thyatira derives its name from the Greek word "daughter." Unhappily enough, the kind of daughter represented in this city's church is a worldly one. Thyatira is a daughter of corruption. The Thyatiran church's defilement is embodied in its association with Jezebel, the worst queen in Israel's history. To Thyatira, Jesus introduces himself as "the Son of God, who hath his eyes like unto a flame of fire, and his feet are like fine brass" (Rev 2:18b). Fire and brass are emblematic of testing and judgment. If they do not stop and think about what they're doing, the Thyatirans are about to be put through judgment. They'll be facing a test. Not all of them will come through it.

As usual, Christ begins with highlighting positive elements of the church. From the opening section of his letter, Thyatira sounds good enough. "I know thy works, and charity, and service, and faith, and thy patience, and thy works; and the last to be more than the first" (Rev 2:19). It seems like a promising start, but again, sadly, the promise is unfulfilled in the state of Thyatira's heart. We quickly learn the Thyatiran church's troubles. The people tolerate a self-proclaimed prophetess, here called Jezebel. Jesus may be naming her Jezebel in order to make a point about her evil words and deeds. The woman here clearly follows the model of the ancient queen Jezebel. Wife of King Ahab of Israel, ancient Jezebel is notorious for her idolatry, murders, and other acts of extreme wickedness (for example, 1 Kgs 16:31; 18:4a, 13a; 21:1–26). She was the daughter of the pagan Sidonian king Ethbaal, and she lived like it, bringing all of her idolatrous conduct to the marriage with Ahab and to her influential role as queen (1 Kgs 16:31). She is a daughter of corruption, just as is her namesake in the daughter city Thyatira.

Thyatira's Jezebel is likewise synonymous with wickedness. She is known for committing and inciting evil deeds and behaviors. She "teach[es]" and "seduc[es]" God's people "to commit fornication, and to eat things sacrificed unto idols" (Rev 2:20b). Given the opportunity to repent, she has refused. As a result, she and her unrepentant fellow adulterers will be cast into great tribulation (Rev 2:22). "And I will kill her children with death; and all the churches shall know that I am he which searcheth the reins and hearts: and I will give unto every one of you according to your works" (Rev 2:23).

Jesus reassures the faithful believers in Thyatira. Those who have stayed pure will have no other burden put upon them. These are the Christians who have refused to believe that they can acquire new powers, abilities, or sacred knowledge from cults and evil activities (Rev 2:24). Rather than gaining temporary goods or earthly influence, the overcomers of Thyatira can expect power over the nations. They will receive the morning star and obtain legitimate authority through the King of kings (Rev 2:27). In rejecting the pagan promises of secret knowledge, sacred power, and diabolical influence, these believers have a far greater, purer future reserved for them.

Corrupt Thyatira is near its destruction and will enter into the condemnation of tribulation and judgment. The faithless in Thyatira should expect trouble if they don't consider their ways and act quickly with repentant hearts. Still, as close as Thyatira is to death, next comes a church already in the throes of its final moments. This is Sardis, a church of death. Speaking to Sardis, Jesus calls himself the One who "hath the seven Spirits of God, and the seven stars" (Rev 3:1). He is the King on his throne, fully God and fully man, ruler of all life. "I know thy works, that thou hast a name that thou livest, and art dead" (Rev 3:1b). Jesus holds the seven churches in his hand. He is their reason for existing. He is their very life.

Knowing what people think of Sardis by reputation, Jesus as God knows the truth about the church there. This church is only nominally alive. The Lord delivers a stark warning to the people: Watch! Find and nurture any life that is left! These remnants of dying faith are "ready to die" (Rev 3:2b). The church is not perfect, whole, or complete in God's eyes. If they will turn to Christ and repent—if they will remember the teachings they originally received and return to truth—if they will wake up and watch, then they have the opportunity for life. Otherwise, they will be caught unawares. "I will come on thee as a thief, and thou shalt not know what hour I will come upon thee" (Rev 3:3b).

As the ancient capital of Lydia, the city of Sardis was already connected with a lack of vigilance. Every time this city fell, the defeat occurred because the people assumed they were too strong, too safe, and too well defended to be taken. The people of Sardis hadn't been watchful, as they should have been. The immensely wealthy king Croesus of Lydia had ruled from Sardis. Legendary for his money and power, he lost everything because he was not cautious. He felt overly secure, and because he and his people arrogantly assumed they were safe from all invaders, the empire of Lydia fell to King Cyrus and the Persians. In light of the city's background, Jesus' words to the church of Sardis are thick with meaning. "Pay attention and watch!" he tells them. Don't be caught in your arrogant assumptions.

Still, some at Sardis remain spiritually alive and have not defiled themselves. The Lord promises that they will walk with him (Rev 3:4). Overcomers of Sardis will be clothed with white robes, the garments reserved for saints made righteous and clean through the blood of the Lamb. Jesus claims these believers as his own. Their names are written in the book of life (Rev 3:5).

Our next church is burgeoning, lively Philadelphia. Founded by two close-knit brothers, this city was placed at the crossroads between the East and West. It was intended to be a missionary city for secular cultures. Philadelphia was designed to facilitate interaction between cultures, spreading Western civilization and language to the East, as well as importing Eastern valuables to the West. The city's location yielded an additional benefit in its exceptionally rich soil. Philadelphian farmers enjoyed special success with their thriving vineyards and other abundant crops. At the same time, Philadelphia's location came at a cost and was not without its disadvantages. The beleaguered city suffered from such extensive, frequent earthquakes and tremors that many first-century citizens chose to live in the fields outside of the city.

In general, Philadelphia's hardships, missionary purposes, and agricultural fame make it an ideal reflection of its church. The Philadelphians may be persecuted, but they persevere, pour their efforts into evangelism, and flourish. They are fruitful soil. The great contrast of a healthy church and a dead or lost one becomes ever clearer when we consider that

Philadelphia succeeds Sardis in this series of letters. Sardis churchgoers are spiritually dead or on the cusp of death; Philadelphian Christians are spiritually alive and bearing excellent fruit.

The church after Philadelphia makes for another piercingly sharp contrast with Philadelphia. The last church of the seven is Laodicea. The name Laodicea etymologically refers to the "people's judgment," designating a church that is driven by its own societal standards for good and evil. The situation of Laodicea can be compared to the events of the book of Judges. During the time of Judges, from about the late fourteenth to mid-eleventh centuries BC, the apostate Israelites did what was right in their own eyes (Judg 21:25). Israel's rebellion against God was defined by their willful decisions to do what they judged right, just, and proper. This definition of apostasy in Judges is all over the place in Laodicea.

To Laodicea, the Lord presents himself as "the Amen, the faithful and true witness, the beginning of the creation of God" (Rev 3:14b). Amen means "let it be," or "so be it." Jesus Christ represents the ultimate "let it be" of God. In him, all prophecies find their fulfillment, all life finds meaning, and all history finds its culmination. "For all the promises of God in him are yea, and in him Amen" (2 Cor 1:20a). Everything that is in God's will, everything that is right, must align with Jesus Christ. Nothing survives or thrives apart from him. According to Colossians, "He is before all things, and by him all things consist" (Col 1:17). The standard of "right in your own eyes" gets us nowhere good, particularly when it comes to anything of substance.

As the faithful and true witness, Jesus is the only way, truth, and life (John 14:6). What he says in Scripture is the road map to heaven. We cannot run away from him or get around him. In the end, conscience, creation, and the Bible testify to the truth of Jesus as the Messiah. In Rev 3, Jesus emphasizes the truth of his identity in the context of Scripture. We have to read the Bible on its own terms and take it as the absolute truth. Nothing else has meaning.

As the beginning of the creation of God, Jesus is One with God. He created everything; he is before everything. Col 1 says, "For by him were all things created" (Col 1:16a). He has eternal preeminence (Col 1:18). With the titles in Rev 3:14, Jesus reminds Laodicea that he is not an ordinary human being or prophet whom they can permanently choose to disagree with or ignore. He's more than just "a good man" or "a guiding light." Contrary to many people's wrongful assertions, Jesus did not come to demonstrate that regular humans can evolve to attain a higher status. His life displays the truth of him as the Messiah, God incarnate.

The Lord knows the Laodiceans' works, but he also knows that their hearts and minds are not devoted to him. Conditions are so extreme that Jesus does not give even one word of commendation to Laodicea. In fact, circumstances are so bad that he's about to spew this church out of his mouth. He will reject the Laodiceans completely because he is so sickened by them.

While these churchgoers believe that they are rich and in great shape, they are far from it. "Thou are wretched, and miserable, and poor, and blind, and naked" (Rev 3:17b), Jesus says. He strictly admonishes the Laodiceans to buy pure gold and white clothing from him. To be wealthy and clothed, they must have authentic wealth and clothing, and they cannot produce those for themselves. Real resources and real garments only come through a genuine relationship with Christ. Jesus' words should have stung the Laodiceans. The city of Laodicea was known for its special wool industry. No clothing? They should have been the source of everyone else's textiles and garments, not to mention their own! Yet Jesus says the opposite, telling the Laodiceans that they are naked and impoverished.

The Lord further commands the Laodiceans to receive eye lotion from him so that they can see clearly. Here, too, Jesus is making another pointed remark. Laodicea was a well-known hub of treatments for eye conditions. It produced medicinal eye lotion. Although the Laodiceans think that they have wonderful vision and enable others to see clearly, their own eyesight is worse than compromised. They need medication for it (Rev 3:18). The eye doctors need the Great Physician to give them sight. As Jesus told the Pharisees, "Now ye say, We see; therefore your sin remaineth" (John 9:41b).

God's words to Laodicea sound harsh, but Jesus reminds the people that he rebukes and chastens those whom he loves. He urges them to repent. He then issues a personal invitation. He's knocking at the door. Anyone who is willing to listen and act has the opportunity to enter into intimacy with him (Rev 3:20). Overcomers from Laodicea have a future promise of intimacy, as well. They can eat with him now, enjoying fellowship in the present. They can physically reign with him in the future, when they join Jesus Christ in his kingdom.

The address to Laodicea concludes with the same instruction that Jesus gives at the end of each letter. "He that hath an ear, let him hear what the Spirit saith unto the churches" (Rev 3:22). Over and over, Christ declares that his words are for everybody. Jesus, the truth, will not be denied. He's speaking. Are we willing to listen?

These, then, are the seven churches. Each one is significant as a cultural center known for something, whether the source of fame is a cult, art, hospital, trade, East-West connections, or another aspect of civilization altogether. Jesus is dictating these letters to John near the end of the first century, at a time when the Roman Empire is continuing to grow and thrive. The Church itself was born not even seventy years before John's writing of Revelation. In this early church culture of Rev 2–3, the Christians still have no idea that there will be almost two thousand more years of history. They're living at a time when persecution has ebbed and waned, is about to intensify again, and will go on across the generations.

As types, the seven churches remain with us in the twenty-first century. Jesus intends for us to be reading, listening, and studying these letters. They are models for us to keep in mind. As models, the five churches of Ephesus, Pergamon, Thyatira, Sardis, and Laodicea are especially sobering. They may look strong and healthy. They may sound good in theory. They may say the right words. But what are they, below the surface? What is the state of the heart beneath? We have to ask: What do these churchgoers claim about Jesus? What do they claim about the Bible? Those key questions are vital for determining their spiritual health. Beyond that, how are they living out their faith? Are they abiding in Jesus? As individuals, in examining our hearts, we have to bear these questions in mind, too. They ought to be with us in everything that we do. Our relationship with Jesus is the most important thing in all of eternity.

Reflection Questions:

1. What are the various levels of application for the letters to the churches in Rev 2–3?
2. Read Rev 1. How does this chapter set up the book by communicating Jesus' authority over heaven and earth?
3. When you read Rev 2, how do the first four churches exhibit different relationships with Jesus as the Lord and Savior?
4. In Rev 3, how do the last three churches display different attitudes toward the Bible as God's Word? Do they see it as the ultimate standard for good and evil?

5. As a whole, all Christians alive today are part of the Church, the Body of Christ (the Church Invisible). But we also talk about the church or churches as an institution or series of institutions, called the Church Visible. Why is it important to recognize a distinction between the Church Invisible and the Church Visible? That is, why do we need to recognize a difference between (*a*) the Body of Christ and (*b*) churches as institutions?

6. How or where do you see elements of all seven of these churches in modern churches, ministries, or other institutions around you?

3

Holiness and Wholeness

> And to the angel of the church in Philadelphia write; These things saith *he that is holy*, he that is true, he that hath the key of David, he that openeth, and no man shutteth; and shutteth, and no man openeth. —Rev 3:7[1]

IF EVERY TITLE THAT Jesus gives himself at the beginning of each letter has a significant meaning for the church he is addressing at the time, what about the opening of the letter to the Philadelphians? From the outset, noticing how Jesus introduces himself in each case gives us insight into this church's relationship with him. What does he tell them about himself, and how does it reflect their intimacy with or distance from him?

The very first thing that Jesus says in the letter to Philadelphia is this: "These things saith he that is holy" (Rev 3:7). His utterance sets the tone for this letter, signifying that Christ's holiness is an underlying, essential trait of his relationship with this church. Jesus' holiness is foundational to his interactions with the Philadelphians. Digging deeper into what holiness means, we can have a clearer picture of why it is so vital to understand what holiness entails. Recognizing that Jesus is holy must be fundamental for us, too.

Notice what the Lord does not say. He does not start the letter by talking about the Philadelphians and *their* holiness. He has to be the starting point for anyone else's holiness, and in this letter, he obviously is. Thus, in

---

1. Italics added.

his introduction, Jesus presents a litmus test that the Philadelphians have already passed. He is holy and righteous. The Philadelphians believe that he is holy and righteous. What does this say about their convictions? They know who Jesus is and who they are not. If Jesus is holy and righteous, then he is no mere man. He cannot be a sinner; he must be perfect by God's standards. The Philadelphians do not have their eyes on themselves and how perfect they are trying to be, but on Jesus and how perfect he already is. They know that being good is not enough, and they obviously do not consider themselves inherently good or equal to Christ.

Jesus' words convey a lot about what the Philadelphians believe and how they function as a church. If they believe that Jesus is holy, then they must believe that he is inherently sinless. For him to be inherently sinless, he must be God. His innate righteousness is a core truth that is the first element of a healthy relationship with Jesus Christ.

In Isa 45, God declares, "There is no God else beside me; a just God and a Saviour; there is none beside me" (Isa 45:21b). He goes on to say, "Look unto me, and be ye saved, all the ends of the earth: for I am God, and there is none else" (Isa 45:22). No one but God is just and all powerful. No one but God is righteous and pure. Psalm 14 pronounces that "there is none that doeth good" (Ps 14:1b), emphasizing, "there is none that doeth good, no, not one" (Ps 14:3b). Paul quotes Ps 14 in Rom 3 as he explains the universality of human sinfulness. He summarizes: "For all have sinned, and come short of the glory of God" (Rom 3:23). Romans 3:23 is one of the verses most often used in evangelism. It's easy to remember, and it gets straight to the point. We're all sinners, all impure. In other words, we are all unholy apart from Jesus.

Holiness, in biblical terms, is an intrinsic attribute of God. He makes us holy when we believe in Jesus as our personal Lord and Savior. But what is holiness? What does it really mean to say that someone or something is holy?

The word "holy" comes from a Proto-Germanic word root that, in turn, comes from a much older Proto-Indo-European root, *kailo-.[2] *Kailo- refers to what is "whole" or "uninjured." It's the same word root that gives us words like "hale" or "healthy." Holiness, accordingly, is the condition of being entire, whole, and sound. The word's etymology indicates how someone who is intrinsically holy is worthy of reverence and worship. A holy person or being is fundamentally complete and independent.

---

2. Watkins, *American Heritage Dictionary*, s.v. "kailo-."

Scripture states that because God alone is intrinsically holy, he alone is worthy of reverence. "O worship the Lord in the beauty of holiness: fear before him, all the earth" (Ps 96:9).

Being holy means that God is *whole* in himself. He does not lack anything. The Lord God is the Father, the Son, and the Spirit, three Persons in One, the Trinity. He is One God, with the singular verb. God is enough in himself. He is entirely complete on his own. In his holiness, he is eternally, unchangingly, and unfailingly whole.

When we accept Jesus as personal Lord and Savior, we partake of his completeness. "And of his fulness have all we received, and grace for grace" (John 1:16). Saying that God is perfect emphasizes his wholeness and completeness. The word "perfect" actually means "complete." God is complete in himself. He is perfect, completely filled up and full, without ever needing anything or anyone else added. He is flawless, more than adequate for any task. He is the very essence of perfection and completion. As a result of God's definitive holiness, the world must compete with him whenever it attempts to find or prove its own holiness. It has to argue that God is not enough—that we are enough without him, and that he's not any better than we are, if he exists at all.

The Bible makes clear that holiness is an active trait. By virtue of its nature, holiness has an impact on its surroundings. The holiness of God is not passive. Think of the effects it has on everyone who even approaches the Lord in Scripture. At the burning bush in the desert, Moses is overwhelmed by God's holiness and, as a consequence, has to stay at a safe distance from the bush. "Put off thy shoes from off thy feet," orders the Lord, "for the place whereon thou standest is holy ground" (Exod 3:5b). Moses hides his face for fear of looking upon the Lord's glory. God's holiness weighs on him.

Later, Exod 19 displays the Lord's holiness before Mount Sinai. The Israelites tremble in fear as God descends upon the mountain: "There were thunders and lightnings, and a thick cloud upon the mount, and the voice of the trumpet exceeding loud" (v. 16b). "And mount Sinai was altogether on a smoke, because the Lord descended upon it in fire: and the smoke thereof ascended as the smoke of a furnace, and the whole mount quaked greatly" (v. 18). The Lord's righteousness here is experienced through multiple senses. It's heard in the unseen trumpet's call, felt in the dreadful earthquakes, and seen in the towering smoke from invisible flames. The people shudder because they are overcome by God's holy presence. Holiness makes and leaves a mark.

Similarly, witnessing the Lord's throne room, the prophet Isaiah is overpowered by God's awesome holiness. As the seraphim cry out with praise for God's holiness, the temple quakes and is filled with smoke (Isa 6:4). Isaiah is smitten. "Woe is me! for I am undone; because I am a man of unclean lips" (6:5a). To purify Isaiah, the seraphim is ordered to bring a live coal from the altar and to touch the coal to the prophet's lips. This act of cleansing signifies the Lord's purification of Isaiah and his speech. Isaiah is sanctified. He is set apart to be a prophet and to present the Lord's message to the people. Only God's merciful holiness allows Isaiah to be clean enough to come before the throne.

Hebrews 12 says that without holiness, no one can see the Lord (v. 14). We cannot stand in front of a bush that burns with God's holy fire, nor can we stand at the foot of a mountain that is set aflame with the barest breath of his holiness. The holiness of God demands purity. The reality of his holiness further accentuates our need for grace. How can any sinful human being dare to approach the Lord? None can. As fallen creatures, we have only one hope, that which is found in Jesus Christ.

God's completeness and perfection as the Holy Trinity are self-sustaining. His wholeness is the same fullness seen in Jesus, because of who he is as God. "For it pleased the Father that in him should all fulness dwell," according to Colossians (Col 1:19).

The fullness of Jesus is shared with us as his Church. The Philadelphians relished Christ's fullness, relying on Jesus as God. Jesus reminded them of the magnitude of his holiness as their purification and salvation when he introduced himself to them as the Holy One. As Col 2 states,

> For in him dwelleth all the fulness of the Godhead bodily. And ye are complete in him, which is the head of all principality and power. (vv. 9–10)

Jesus' completeness as the Son of God is a defining characteristic. He has always been and always will be holy. In becoming Christians, we become holy through him. His holiness becomes *our* defining characteristic. This is why the Philadelphians could not have been surprised or offended at Jesus' introduction to them in Rev 3. He was drawing attention to the heart of their relationship with him. Everything that they had and were in Jesus depended on his essential character and identity as the unchanging, perfect God.

In 1 Peter, Peter speaks of the separation between what Christians were before salvation and what we are meant to be now that we are saved. "But as he which hath called you is holy, so be ye holy in all manner of conversation" (1:15). The word "conversation" in the King James Version is the translation of a Greek word that means "lifestyle" and "way of living." It has to do with our conduct and attitudes as much as with our speech and dialogue. Peter is reminding us that we are meant to be holy in both our words and our works, not in either the one or the other. Christianity, he's saying, is comprehensive, not compartmentalized.

Moreover, 1 Peter again explains why we should be holy: "Because it is written, Be ye holy; for I am holy" (1:16). This quotation comes from the Old Testament. And it comes not only from one verse in the Old Testament but multiple passages! The Lord often speaks of his holiness. Every time he speaks, we need to be listening. If God says something more than once, then we ought to make sure that we're paying attention. He is telling us something big and important. Holiness is no exception. With God, it's the rule, because he is the very definition of holiness.

Specifically, the words "be holy for I am holy" first appear in Lev 11. In this chapter, God has just given the Israelites a list of rules about what they can eat. The list divides living things into categories of "clean" and "unclean." Mammals, insects, fish, birds, reptiles—it's a pretty full list, distinguishing between all kinds of creatures. For example, camels and rabbits were not clean to eat, because they do not have divided hooves (vv. 4, 6). They are considered unclean. Pigs have divided hooves, but they do not chew their cud, and clean animals are ones that chew the cud *and* have divided hooves (vv. 3, 7). Therefore, pigs are unclean. Nor were all fish clean or unclean. A fish had to have fins *and* scales in order to be considered clean (vv. 9–12). Additionally, the Lord goes through a long list of birds that are unclean and not to be consumed as food. The list includes eagles, vultures, ravens, owls, swans, storks, and more (vv. 13–19). Beyond that, there are other unclean creatures to be avoided, such as weasels, tortoises, mice, ferrets, snails, and moles, to name a few (vv. 29–30).

Why would God set such strict standards about what the people could eat? What is the significance of Lev 11, and what does it have to do with the Lord's holiness? First, these rules about clean and unclean foods were hygienic. These standards protected the people's health, especially important for a time when the Israelites had poorer access to clean water and sterile cooking tools. Second, these standards helped the people live out their obedience. By adhering to these restrictions, the people could show that they were interested in doing what the Lord would have them do. Following dietary rules under the Mosaic law was one method of investing in their relationship with him.

On a wider scale, the standards of clean and unclean foods in Lev 11 reflect a broader context of holiness. The rules here offer more details that show truths about God's character. There are reasons behind each category of creature's inclusion and status as clean or unclean. Notice how vital it is for the people simply to recognize that the labels "clean" and "unclean" exist. They need to know that not everything is safe and pure to eat or to touch. Certain creatures are an abomination to eat. As the Lord says,

> For I am the LORD your God: ye shall therefore sanctify yourselves, and ye shall be holy; for I am holy: neither shall ye defile yourselves with any manner of creeping thing that creepeth upon the earth. For I am the LORD that bringeth you up out of the land of Egypt, to be your God: ye shall therefore be holy, for I am holy. (vv. 44–45)

Later in Leviticus, before giving various other essential laws about proper conduct and idolatry, God says it again: "Ye shall be holy: for I the LORD your God am holy" (Lev 19:2b). He is not telling the people to do anything he cannot do. Righteousness means perfection, and perfection means existing according to unchanging standards of the absolutely highest purity. God does not make mistakes. Jesus proves God's perfection. As God in the flesh, he lived a perfect, sinless life. He "did not sin, neither was guile found in his mouth" (1 Pet 2:22). The Lord gives these standards because absolute cleanliness and righteousness are entailed in holiness.

In commanding the people to separate themselves from dallying with any and all forms of sorcery, witchcraft, idolatry, and necromancy, the Lord yet again commands them to be pure. "Sanctify yourselves therefore, and be ye holy: for I am the LORD your God" (Lev 20:7). He continues, "And ye shall keep my statues, and do them: I am the LORD which sanctify you" (Lev 20:8).

The key to our sanctification is the Lord's holiness. "I am the LORD which sanctify you." Apart from the power of God, it is completely impossible to be holy as God is holy. People can never sanctify themselves through human behaviors or activities. The Lord can make us righteous, but we are not able to make ourselves righteous. We cannot even come close to being righteous on our own. Holiness, as we see here, involves what we do *and* how we live. It maintains rigid standards of perfection and absolute purity.

Holiness involves being set apart in every single aspect. Just as in ancient Israel, where it was the Lord who accomplished sanctification, sanctification today for us as sinful human beings still requires dependence on God. He is the single source of sanctification. The Old Testament exhibits the truth of holiness and sanctification through God alone, in expectant faith that he alone can provide the atonement that will make us holy. The New Testament reveals the Messiah in the flesh, showing that our dependence is on God in the face of Jesus Christ. Our faith finds fulfillment in Jesus. We have to rely on him to be freed from the curse of sin and death. Hebrews says that, by sacrificing himself, Jesus "perfected for ever them that are sanctified" (Heb 10:14b). He is our perfection. In Matt 5, Jesus states, "Be ye therefore perfect, even as your Father which is in heaven is perfect" (v. 48). We are complete solely through Christ. In turn, we act on faith in the completion we have through him.

In the Philadelphian letter, Jesus affirms his own identity and underscores the nature of his relationship with the Philadelphian Christians. He's not merely letting the Philadelphians make an assumption about him or decide how they feel about who he is. Indeed, in declaring that he is holy, Jesus is declaring that he is God. The Philadelphians realize that he is God, and because they realize that truth, they have no issue with his calling himself holy. Their identification as Christians begins and ends with Christ.

The Bible constantly speaks of holiness together with sanctification and our relationship with God, as evident in the verses from Leviticus: "Sanctify yourselves therefore, and be ye holy" (20:7a), for example, or "I am the Lord which sanctify you" (20:8b). The English word "sanctification" is a compound formed from the two Latin roots *sanctus*, "holy," and *facere*, "to make." Sanctification is a consecration or "making holy" of someone or something. Coming from the same word root as "sanctification," the term "saint" connotes the process of consecration. Saints are those who have been made holy, who have been and are being sanctified. They are people consecrated and set apart by the Lord, as Peter explains to fellow believers in 1 Peter.

Putting consecration and the concept of "set apart" in perspective, Christians' holiness begins with the acknowledgment that, on our own, we are unholy. In coming to Jesus, we are coming to terms with the self-deceptive weight of our own sin. First John 1:8 reads, "If we say that we have no sin, we deceive ourselves, and the truth is not in us." If you believe you are a sinner, then you cannot believe that you're holy, because if you are a sinner, then you are not perfect. You are not righteous. Logically, if you are to become holy, then you need someone holy to sanctify you and cleanse you of your sins.

Thus, to become a Christian, you have to recognize Jesus as the Holy One. Because he is holy, he is able to cleanse you and remove your unholiness. In living a Christian life, you celebrate his holiness. By contrast, false religions of all sorts argue for other means of holiness. They allege that good works, social advancement, self-evolution, legalism, and other things are roads to heaven. But these belief systems go blatantly against the truth of the Bible. They deny who Jesus is, insisting that we are already holy or can make ourselves holy without him. In other words, they insist that we can either erase our own sins or that we never had any sins in the first place.

First John settles the issue. When we say we have no sin, we are not walking in the truth. We cannot be in the truth if we deny our own sinful nature. In spite of our sin, however, there is a way forward that involves acknowledging the truth of who and what we are as sinners. John writes, "If we confess our sins, he is faithful and just to forgive our sins, and to cleanse us from all unrighteousness" (1:9). God provides a way to heaven, all right, and the Philadelphians knew it. They knew that Jesus is the Holy One.

Christ's holiness made him different from any other person. Being God in the flesh, he was different from the beginning, before time began! When we come to him, he makes us different from other people, too, and even from ourselves. He rescues us from unholiness, delivering us by his own mercy and grace. When we accept him, he shares his fullness with us, so that we find our completion in him. In that sense, being holy implies actions on our parts and on his. Holiness is never passive. It always has a lasting impact. The Philadelphians understood the weight of holiness. Jesus' words to them reflect their understanding. These people lived lives that were an active, ongoing pursuit of holiness. They were following the Holy One. They counted on him. When Jesus introduced himself, they knew exactly who he was, by name.

Reflection Questions:

1. Why is it so important that we understand that we're unholy—that we're sinners?

2. Ephesians 2 describes the fundamental change that takes place when we're saved. What does this show us about the relationship between holiness and spiritual life?

3. What does holiness look like in the everyday Christian life?

4. How does Jesus model holiness for us?

5. Holiness is sanctification that sets us apart from what we once were, as well as from the appetites of the world. What practical habits can you develop with the specific goal of aligning your desires with God's? Name two ways you can adjust your routine to "recalibrate" your thinking during the day. Some ideas might include meditating on God's Word by carrying verses on note cards for a quick glance (Ps 1); choosing someone to pray for privately by name, asking the Lord to show you how to love that person as he does (1 Pet 1:22); or committing to a set time when you will regularly listen to praise and worship music (Ps 104:33).

6. The first song in the Bible is Exod 15, Israel's song of praise after God parts the Red Sea and delivers the Jews from the Egyptian army. How does this song express appreciation for God and his holiness?

4

The Bedrock of Truth

> And to the angel of the church in Philadelphia write; These things saith he that is holy, *he that is true*, he that hath the key of David, he that openeth, and no man shutteth; and shutteth, and no man openeth. —Rev 3:7[1]

"He that is true." That is the second part of Christ's introduction to Philadelphia. Jesus has already established that he is the Holy One. Only those who humble themselves to acknowledge that he is holy and that they are not can bask in his holiness, since they are willing to accept his title as the One "that is true." The Philadelphians operate under humility. They know that God is righteous, and that they are not. They are well prepared to embrace him as the Truth.

What about truth? What are the implications of the declaration that Jesus is true, and why would the Philadelphians be supposed to pay any particular attention to Jesus as the One who is true? It plainly matters enough for Jesus to mention it at the beginning of the letter. Why is it so important to God to identify Jesus as true?

In John 14, Jesus bluntly tells his disciples that he is "the way, the truth, and the life: no man cometh unto the Father, but by me" (v. 6b). On the face of it, his statement is an utterly brazen claim. After all, Jesus is not asserting that he's a nice, normal man who can offer a suggestion or two about what is right or wrong. He is not calling himself a human prophet with some special

---

1. Italics added.

connection to divine secrets, nor is he alleging that he's an ordinary person who's now spiritually evolved into a higher being. No, Jesus is not just saying that he *knows* the truth. He proclaims that he *is* the Truth.

The concept of "truth," much less "Truth" with a capital *T*, is an uncomfortable one for many people today. Modern Western civilization is obsessed with "relative truth." Absolute truth says there is the Truth. Relative truth is the opposite idea. It proclaims, "That's true for you, but not true for me." Relative truth asserts that there are no absolute truths. According to relative truth, nothing is absolutely true for everybody. Every truth depends on what someone feels and wants. You can believe something, and it can be your truth. Somebody else may disagree with you and hold an entirely different truth that is supposedly equally true.

Relative truth comes with a whole set of logical problems. A major issue is that relative truth is itself deceptive. "True for me, but not for you" is an absolute statement. It declares that something that is true for one person is *absolutely* not always true for everybody else. When relativists use this absolute statement to argue against absolute truth, they're using an absolute truth to argue that absolute truths don't exist. Therefore, relative truth cannot be true, because it would be an absolute truth. And if it represents an absolute truth, then absolute truths exist, so relative truth cannot be accurate. From the beginning, relative truth is illogical and impractical. It debunks itself.

Ironically enough, relative truth serves as an excellent cover for slipping in a *different* absolute truth, one that runs counter to Scripture. This antibiblical substitute, while claiming to be all-welcoming and all-affirming, is really just another way to try to deny God. It argues that, whatever you want to believe, it is *absolutely* wrong (again, supposedly) to believe that the God of the Bible is who and what he says he is. According to relative truth, you can choose to believe anything that you want to believe, except for believing that the Bible is true. Biblical truth in strictly biblical terms becomes utterly off-limits. Relative truth claims that Scripture in the Bible's own context is hateful, narrow-minded, and absolutely unacceptable. Hence, being self-contradictory and rebellious, relative truth proclaims that truth can be absolutely anything except for Scripture.

Notably, the veneer of relative truth as "relative truth" becomes less necessary for the world as paganism and apostasy increase. In the last days, humanity will supply itself with another more overt kind of absolute truth in worship of Satan and a new world order (as witnessed in Rev 13, among other places). Relative truth is helping to pave the way for the very last days of our age.

In a world that says truth can be anything except Christianity, we must constantly return to the vital question of what truth is. The Philadelphians had to go through the same thought process as they considered truth. They lived in a world of competing worldviews and multitudes of cults, all of which claimed to possess truth of some kind. What did truth mean? Like us, the church of Philadelphia had to be constantly on guard against falsehoods. Like us, they had to ask themselves what truth was, and they ended up concluding that truth is Jesus Christ. In any century or age, Jesus does not work with relative truth. He deals in bedrock absolutes. As the Rock, he is the Absolute Truth. In saying that he is the Truth, he is making an absolute statement in Rev 3, just as he did in John 14. As short as it is, the identifier "he that is true" in Rev 3 defines who Jesus is and what he does.

The very idea of truth is naturally bound up in absolutes. The word "truth" actually traces back to an ancient root for "tree." "Tree" traces back to a word root for something that is firm.[2] The English word "truth" therefore means something that stands firm. It is a solid foundation that does not move, shake, bend, or fall apart. By definition, Truth is an absolute, fixed principle. Truth is found in facts that can be trusted to stand and keep standing.

In claiming to be the Truth, Jesus presents himself as the firm, unchanging foundation, trustworthy and faithful in every circumstance. His faithfulness is a crucial aspect of his character, calling attention to his Godhood. Throughout the Old Testament, the Lord identifies himself as the only One who can be trusted to do what he says he will do. He can be trusted to do what he will do in the future because he has done what he said he would do in the past. He's given prophecies over and over in history, telling what happens before the fact in order to prove that he knows what is coming. In Isaiah, for instance, the Lord repeatedly shows that he knows the beginning, end, and everything in the middle.

> And who, as I, shall call, and shall declare it, and set it in order for me, since I appointed the ancient people? and the things that are coming, and shall come, let them shew unto them. Fear ye not, neither be afraid: have not I told thee from that time, and have declared it? ye are even my witnesses. Is there a God beside me? yea, there is no God; I know not any. (44:7–8)

2. Watkins, *American Heritage Dictionary*, s.v. "deru-."

> Assemble yourselves and come; draw near together, ye that are escaped of the nations: they have no knowledge that set up the wood of their graven image, and pray unto a god that cannot save. Tell ye, and bring them near; yea, let them take counsel together: who hath declared this from ancient time? who hath told it from that time? have not I the LORD? and there is no God else beside me; a just God and a Saviour; there is none beside me. (45:20–21)

The Lord challenges Israel: Can their false gods accurately foretell events? Can these supposed deities declare anything or provide any reasons why anyone should rely on them? The answer is repeatedly no. The pagan gods are frauds. Some are demons attempting to steal God's worship for themselves. Others are blocks of wood, pieces of stone, or other human inventions. They cannot replace the Almighty God. Demons may be able to orchestrate "fulfillments" of small prophecies or might have human agents arranging events to make false gods look real, but they are frauds and fakes, propped up by deception. By contrast, the Lord God, the God of the Bible, stands up to every test. He is solid, firm, and faithful. He is true.

> Let them bring them forth, and shew us what shall happen: let them shew the former things, what they be, that we may consider them, and know the latter end of them; or declare us things for to come. Shew the things that are to come hereafter, that we may know that ye are gods: yea, do good, or do evil, that we may be dismayed, and behold it together. (Isa 41:22–23)

All of these verses emphasize the importance of who Jesus is. When he calls himself the Truth, he is saying that he is God incarnate, and that he is faithful, true, solid, and unchanging. If Jesus is not God, then his words are downright blasphemous. If he is God, then his declaration is a judgment upon all those who would deny him. Either way, we all face the choice of how we will respond to what Jesus says. Whoever you are, you have to make a decision about how you'll react to Jesus' claims. Biblically, the only positive response is to come to Jesus as Lord and Savior. This is acceptance of Jesus for who he is. Spiritually, it's having our eyes opened at last. We gain true sight.

The contrast between spiritual sight and spiritual blindness is exhibited throughout the Bible. It is a basic distinction that extends to every human being who has ever lived. An excellent illustration of the difference between seeing the truth or being blind to it is found in John 18. In this chapter, Pontius Pilate is interrogating Jesus prior to the crucifixion. Pilate asks Jesus outright: What crime has Jesus committed? Why have the Jews brought Jesus to trial? Jesus' reply is anything but a traditional defense.

> Jesus answered, My kingdom is not of this world: if my kingdom were of this world, then would my servants fight, that I should not be delivered to the Jews: but now is my kingdom not from hence. Pilate therefore said unto him, Art thou a king then? Jesus answered, Thou sayest that I am a king. To this end was I born, and for this cause came I into the world, that I should bear witness unto the truth. Every one that is of the truth heareth my voice. Pilate saith unto him, What is truth? And when he had said this, he went out again unto the Jews, and saith unto them, I find in him no fault at all. (vv. 36–38)

In the conversation between Jesus and Pilate, several significant events took place. Unpeeling the layers, we come to see Jesus as the Philadelphian Christians must have understood him when he told them who he was.

First, Jesus said he was born to bear witness to the truth. He elaborates on his witness in John 5, where he tells the Jews that he has come to do the Father's will. Jesus adds that the Father has sent him (John 5:30). "If I bear witness of myself, my witness is not true" (John 5:31). No man should be able to declare himself God or the Messiah without proof. Jesus certainly did not. He had more than enough proof to back him up and show who he was. He offered that proof repeatedly.

The law and prophets, the ministry of John the Baptist, the words of the Father, and the evidence of the Holy Spirit all bore witness to who Jesus was. He fulfilled every prophecy and lived a perfect life in accordance with the law. Everything in Scripture identified him as the long-awaited Messiah, the Christ (Luke 24:25–27). If Jesus had simply come and announced that he was the Christ without anything else to support his claim, then the disciples would not and should not have accepted him as the Messiah. As it was, he fulfilled all righteousness and demonstrated exactly who he was.

Joining Jesus in proclaiming Jesus the Christ, John the Baptist testified that Jesus was the Lamb of God who "taketh away the sin of the world" (John 1:29b). Jesus reminds the Jews that John told them he was the Messiah. "Ye sent unto John, and he bare witness unto the truth" (John 5:33). Four hundred years earlier, the prophet Malachi had foretold that the Messiah would be preceded by another prophet, one who would come in the spirit of Elijah. "Behold, I will send you Elijah the prophet before the coming of the great and dreadful day of the Lord" (Mal 4:5). This prophetic predecessor was meant to make hearts ready for the Lord: "Behold, I will send my messenger, and he shall prepare the way before me," the Lord declares (Mal 3:1a). Later, Jesus explains, "For all the prophets and the law prophesied until John. And if ye will receive it, this is Elias, which was for to come" (Matt 11:13–14). John came to awaken minds and hearts to their need for salvation through Jesus Christ.

Even so, Jesus does not rely solely on John for a personal reference. John is not the only one to confirm Jesus' identity. Christ pronounces, "But I receive not testimony from man. . . . But I have greater witness than that of John: for the works which the Father hath given me to finish, the same works that I do, bear witness of me, that the Father hath sent me" (John 5:34a, 36). The Messiah was required to validate himself by performing a whole litany of certain miracles and other deeds, all of which Jesus did. He necessarily fulfilled "all righteousness" (Matt 3:15).

In the Sermon on the Mount, Jesus states that he comes to fulfill the law and prophets (Matt 5:17). He performed so many works that multitudes of the people were compelled to believe. They were astonished, asking, "When Christ cometh, will he do more miracles than these which this man hath done?" (John 7:31b). Other observers declared, "John did no miracle: but all things that John spake of this man were true" (John 10:41b). Early in Jesus' ministry, the disciple Nathanael expresses amazement at Christ's foreknowledge. Jesus seems to answer with gentle amusement at how easily Nathanael is impressed. Christ makes a promise to the astounded disciple: "Thou shalt see greater things than these" (John 1:50b). Throughout his earthly ministry alone, Jesus lived up to the promise he made to Nathanael. Christ worked countless amazing miracles. Kings heard of him and hoped to see him perform miracles as if his wonders were magic tricks (Mark 6:14, Luke 23:8). Kings like Herod never reached the right conclusion about who Jesus was, but the works were a witness for those who were willing to see clearly (John 10:38).

Additionally, God the Father testifies to who Jesus is. The Father affirmed Jesus as the Son at Jesus' baptism (Matt 3:17) and at the transfiguration (Matt 17:5). Everything Jesus did was in obedience to and in alignment with the Father's will (John 5:19, 36–37). "I am one that bear witness of myself, and the Father that sent me beareth witness of me" (John 8:18). In John 5, Jesus says, "I can of mine own self do nothing: as I hear, I judge: and my judgment is just; because I seek not mine own will, but the will of the Father which hath sent me" (v. 30). Jesus' every action is focused on what God has sent him to do (John 10:25), as confirmed by God the Father on multiple occasions in the Gospels.

If emotions and unfounded allegations were the only so-called "evidence" we ever had, any con artist could claim to be the Messiah. Anyone could arrange to have someone like John as a right-hand man. Someday, a false messiah and his prophet, biblically known as the Antichrist and his false prophet, will do just that. Yet that is not what Jesus did, nor is it all John was. John the Baptist had to fit certain specifications, just as Jesus did. John's ministry is but a single example of the countless fulfilled prophecies related to Jesus as the Christ. The requirements for Jesus as the Messiah were, putting it mildly, extremely stringent. From birth through life to death and resurrection, the Messiah had to meet very precise criteria. The external witness of John was one of many prerequisites for Jesus' messianic ministry.

Messianic prophecy is an objective measurement of who Jesus is as the Messiah. A remarkably specific and detailed type of prophecy, messianic prophecy represents a massive body of information about Christ. All of these prophecies were given hundreds or thousands of years prior to Jesus' birth. Messianic prophecy dictates who the Messiah has to be and what he has to do at certain times in certain places. Jesus repeatedly says, "Search the scriptures; for in them ye think ye have eternal life: and they are they which testify of me" (John 5:39). He challenges the Jews to look to their own prophecies and Scripture. "For had ye believed Moses, ye would have believed me; for he wrote of me" (John 5:46).

In all of these things and more, Jesus proclaims that he embodies the firm foundation of absolute truth. He provides objective evidence to support his claims. The Philadelphian Christians understood Jesus as he presented himself and as Scripture proves him to be. They depended on Jesus as the unchanging standard for holiness, goodness, and righteousness. Because God is faithful and Jesus is God, the Philadelphians realized the need to base their lives and eternities on the words of Jesus Christ. They depended on Jesus as God. If we are going to be Philadelphian Christians, if we are going to be Christians at all, then the truth of who Jesus is remains an absolute non-negotiable for us, as well. It is an essential. We have to take Jesus Christ on his terms, not ours.

Jesus' words to Pilate reflect all of these layers of meaning, displaying who Jesus is and why he has come. But there's more. The next layer to the John 18 interrogation scene before Pilate is that those who are of the truth hear what Jesus has to say, as we see that Philadelphian Christians must.

In John 5, when Jesus challenges the Jews and their leaders, he asks them, "But if ye believe not his writings, how shall ye believe my words?" (v. 47). They cannot claim to follow the truth of Scripture without tumbling into the truth of Jesus. Jesus tells believers that they must abide in him and what he says to be his disciples. Once they do, they will know truth, and the truth will set them free (John 8:32).

Jesus ties truth to God the Son—that is, to himself: "If the Son therefore shall make you free, ye shall be free indeed" (John 8:36). He provokes the Jews to anger when he identifies God as his Father (John 8:42). "And because I tell you the truth, ye believe me not" (John 8:45). Anyone of God, he says, will hear God's words (John 8:47). To be of the truth, we have to listen to the truth and humble ourselves before it. Our doctrine as Christians must be entirely guided by Scripture. We must humble ourselves before Jesus as the Christ, as God in the flesh. His sheep hear his voice, believe in him, and know him. They follow him and receive eternal life through him (John 10:26–27).

In the Gospels, Jesus repeatedly draws a line in the sand. Every single human being must make a choice about him. Will we hear his words and accept him, or not? The truth is exclusive: "I am the way, the truth, and the life: no man cometh unto the Father, but by me" (John 14:6b). As we'll see in upcoming chapters, the exclusivity of truth fuels the Philadelphian devotion to evangelism. To be truly dedicated to missions, the Philadelphians first must believe in the truth behind the mission. Otherwise, what is there to evangelize? What truth is there to be spread?

Finally, we have the visual aspect of a response to truth as demonstrated in John 18, a fitting capstone to any discussion of truth. "Every one that is of the truth heareth my voice," Jesus tells Pilate (v. 37b). Pilate's answer is a patent demonstration of the exclusivity of Jesus and truth in practice. Rather than recognizing what Jesus is saying—rather than hearing the Lord's words and acknowledging them with an open heart—Pilate asks a question that shows how he has missed the entire point of Jesus: "What is truth?" he asks. Having posed the question, Pilate then turns his back and goes outside. Although he has been face to face with Truth incarnate, Pilate does not see. He refuses to see. Instead, he turns his back on Jesus, therefore turning his back on Truth, and deliberately walks away (v. 38).

Each of us has the same choice as Pilate did in that moment. Truth is standing in our very presence. In our generation, Truth stands before us with a name. He is the Messiah who has already come and died for our sins, rising again on the third day. We know the name Jesus Christ. We know his claims. We have a written Bible that claims to be the Word of God. Basically, we have an ultimate claim to truth. It's right in front of us in the face of Jesus Christ. What are we going to do about it? The Philadelphian response is obvious. For them, it's a given that Jesus is the Truth. He introduces himself to Philadelphia as the Truth, knowing the people of the church there know who's speaking to them. Christianity inherently recognizes Jesus as the Truth and relies on him to be the true and faithful Savior. To be Philadelphian, we have to continue embracing that truth, clinging to the facts of who Jesus is by abiding in him and pursuing a closer and closer relationship with him.

Reflection Questions:

1. Why was it so important that Jesus did everything prophecy said he was supposed to do? How does prophecy relate to the truth of who Jesus is?

2. Read John 14. How does receiving Jesus as Lord and Savior allow us to enter into a relationship with him? (See especially vv. 21–23.)

3. Looking back at Gen 3, we see that the serpent convinced Eve that truth was relative, because God's truth was not absolute. How did the satanic deception seduce Eve to turn her back on truth?

4. What does truth look like in our daily walks with Christ?

5. What does truth look like in our interactions with the world? For instance, where do you see the friction between truth and falsehood? Where is it most important that we recognize how worldly "truths" do not match what the Bible says is true?

6. What steps can you take today to cling more closely to truth—specifically, how can you by strengthen your biblical roots and connection to Scripture? For example, you might consider asking an accountability partner to read a certain passage with you every day, or if you have not read the entire Bible, committing to a program to start reading it a chapter at a time.

5

The King and His Keys

And to the angel of the church in Philadelphia write; These things saith he that is holy, he that is true, *he that hath the key of David*, he that openeth, and no man shutteth; and shutteth, and no man openeth. —Rev 3:7[1]

PRESENTING HIMSELF AS HOLY and true, Jesus pronounces that he is "he that hath the key of David" (Rev 3:7). He has affirmed that he is the pure, perfect Lord and that he is absolute truth. The Philadelphians know him as the God who does not change across the ages. What does it mean now to say that he has the key of David?

The phrase "key of David" has significant ramifications for the past, present, and future. In itself, a key symbolizes authority and access. The person who possesses the key to a certain door is the one who determines who can or cannot pass through that door. He has a power that someone without the key does not have. It's not as easy as thinking that someone can simply break the door down. In spiritual terms, a well-built house and a well-prepared homeowner are an unassailable combination.

The key of David is more remarkable than other keys of authority. In 2 Sam 7, God makes a vow to David. After David's death, a Davidic descendant to come will receive a lasting kingdom. "I will stablish the throne of his kingdom for ever" (v. 13b). David's kingship was going to pass down to an eternal king with eternal power. "And thine house and

---

1. Italics added.

thy kingdom shall be established for ever before thee: thy throne shall be established for ever" (2 Sam 7:16).

While a key is meaningful as a general symbol of authority and access, the key to the house of David is even more so. Whoever holds this key has the God-given control of David's kingdom. In uttering this promise to David, the Lord is proclaiming a wider promise that has to do with the Messiah's everlasting purpose and importance. The Messiah, the Christ, was the One chosen and sent by God. As early as Gen 3, prophecies about the Messiah foretell that he will destroy the curse of sin and death that began at the fall of man in the garden of Eden (v. 15).[2]

In Jer 33, God reaffirms that the Messiah will be a descendant of David and an eternal king. "For thus saith the LORD; David shall never want a man to sit upon the throne of the house of Israel" (v. 17). The only way that the promise with David might be broken would be if someone could override God's covenant of day, night, and seasons (vv. 20–21, 25–26). Ps 89 declares that David's throne will endure "as the days of heaven" (v. 29b).

The key of the house of David can only go to the Messiah. Once it is in the Messiah's hands, he possesses the key forever. By saying that he holds the key of David, Jesus again asserts that he is the Messiah. He fulfills all the past promises about what the Messiah will be and do. Additionally, he makes another future promise that looks forward to well beyond today or any earthly kingdom. Christ is the *eternal* King. The Philadelphians can expect that the Messiah will reign forever on David's throne. Jesus' birth announcement from the angel Gabriel confirms Messianic kingship:

> He shall be great, and shall be called the Son of the Highest: and the Lord God shall give unto him the throne of his father David: And he shall reign over the house of Jacob for ever; and of his kingdom there shall be no end. (Luke 1:32–33)

Jesus' tenure as the legitimate ruler of Israel and of the heavenly kingdom will never run out. Being the Messiah, he is the long-awaited King of kings. The truth of Jesus' eternal kingship is one that we as Christians can

---

2. The term "fall of man" refers to the first sin committed by human beings. Despite God's command not to eat from the tree of the knowledge of good and evil, Adam and Eve knowingly break the one law (Gen 3:6). Once in a fallen state of sin, they need a perfect atonement to bridge the gap between them and God. The Messiah is a pure offering for sins. "By mercy and truth iniquity is purged" (Prov 16:6a). The Messiah embodies the Lord's mercy and truth. He deserves to be king, and will one day visibly reign from the throne of Jerusalem (Ps 2).

hold dear and celebrate. Jesus holds the key of David. He is the promised Messiah and the coming King.

In the promise of the Messiah and the example of the key of David, Jesus declares that he has the authority of the eternal kingdom. Still, there is another aspect of the key of David. The key is tied to intentional stewardship. The reference in Rev 3 is not an obscure allusion to the Old Testament. It is a direct quote, coming from Isa 22, and it has its own intentional, significant context.

Isaiah 22 was written in the eighth century BC, long after the ancient nation Israel had already split into two kingdoms. The northern kingdom (Israel) fell into wickedness quickly and went into captivity for its sins. Israel was taken by Assyria before Isaiah received this message from the Lord. At the time of Isaiah's prophecy, the southern kingdom (Judah) is still standing. Judah long outlasts Isaiah himself. In fact, Judah's capital Jerusalem won't be destroyed for over a hundred years after Isaiah's prophecy. However, the Jews in Jerusalem don't know that. They don't have a calendar listing the exact date when Judah will be allowed to fall. They only know that they are under attack from Assyria, the same brutal superpower that has defeated the northern kingdom of Israel and scores of other nations and peoples. For King Hezekiah of Judah and the besieged city of Jerusalem, it is an especially trying time. The encroaching Assyrian army only seems to be gaining more power.

In the midst of such a tumultuous period, God provides an important illustration of messianic sovereignty and character. His message shows not only what the Messiah will be, but also the type of heart God seeks in his people. Hezekiah's treasurer is a man named Shebna. As the chief steward of David's house, Shebna is the man who currently holds the key of the household. He acts as Hezekiah's representative. Shebna is otherwise unknown in Scripture. (He might appear later, in 2 Kgs 18–19 and Isa 36–37. There, *if* this is the same Shebna, he has lost his steward position and is a scribe still awaiting the judgment God pronounced upon him in Isa 22.)

Shebna is a negative example. As unfavorably described in Isa 22, he is the epitome of an extremely disapproved steward. Shebna has been misusing his authority. He's been building a magnificent tomb for himself rather than carrying out his duties for the good of Jerusalem and David's house. God condemns Shebna's actions: "What hast thou here? and whom hast thou here, that thou hast hewed thee out a sepulchre here, as he that heweth him out a sepulchre on high, and that graveth an habitation for himself in a rock?" (Isa 22:16). Although it was not unusual for kings, dignitaries, and other influential elites to build tombs for themselves in the ancient world, Shebna is not a king, and he is not using his influence as he is supposed to be. When he should be helping the king turn the people back to God in order to escape judgment, Shebna is invested in advancing his own career and legacy. His attention is turned in a very wrong direction.

Because Shebna's heart is set on glorifying himself, God is going to remove him from the role of steward and send him into captivity (Isa 22:17–19). Shebna will die far away from the splendid, expensive tomb he is building. The time and money he's foolishly spent will come to nothing. His planning is in vain. We might compare Shebna to the rich man in the parable of Luke 12. In Luke 12:16–21, the wealthy man observes his own wealth and invests everything in physical resources. Devoting his life to empty luxuries and carousing, he never stops to consider the sinful state of his soul or his spiritual poverty before the Lord. "But God said unto him, Thou fool, this night thy soul shall be required of thee: then whose shall those things be, which thou has provided?" (v. 20). The summary of the parable in Luke 12 is much like the situation of Shebna. "So is he that layeth up treasure for himself, and is not rich toward God" (v. 21).

Shebna is the picture of a faithless steward. Enriching himself and concentrating on his personal ambition, he is impoverished toward God and others. He's not supporting the cause of Hezekiah the king or of the Lord, the King of kings. Instead, Shebna advocates for his personal legacy, attempting to create his own glory and fame. While Judah battles for survival and struggles against its own spiritual decay, Shebna is only concerned with himself.

At the same time as God censures Shebna's disgraceful behavior, the Lord has prepared a faithful steward to serve as a positive role model. The Lord names this other man as Shebna's successor:

> And it shall come to pass in that day, that I will call my servant Eliakim the son of Hilkiah: And I will clothe him with thy robe, and strengthen him with thy girdle, and I will commit thy government into his hand: and he shall be a father to the inhabitants of Jerusalem, and to the house of Judah. And the key of the house of David will I lay upon his shoulder; so he shall open, and none shall shut; and he shall shut, and none shall open. (Isa 22:20–22)

If this promise from Isa 22 sounds familiar, it should. It's the same promise we've just seen in Jesus' words in Rev 3. Jesus is the One who permanently holds the key of David. He is both the King and the Steward. As manager of the Lord's household, he controls the access to it. Unlike Shebna, however, Jesus executes the stewardship faithfully and diligently.

In Isa 22, the words of the prophecy relate directly to a man named Eliakim. Eliakim foreshadows the Messiah's faithful stewardship. By 2 Kgs 18, Eliakim has become steward, as foretold by Isaiah (vv. 18, 37). Eliakim is obviously an honorable man. The Lord calls him "my servant" (Isa 22:20b). What nobler accolade could a person receive? Eliakim's name even means "God raises up."[3]

Another interesting feature about Eliakim is that we know his father's name. Eliakim is the son of Hilkiah. This would seem to be a minor detail, but it's remarkable in its own right. We know nothing at all about Eliakim's father, except through Eliakim. For comparison, recall the words of Jesus as he talks about our relationship with the Father and with himself. We can only know God the Father through Jesus the Son. "No man knoweth the Son, but the Father; neither knoweth any man the Father, save the Son, and he to whomsoever the Son will reveal him" (Matt 11:27b). Elsewhere, in John 14, Jesus explains that no one can know the Father without first knowing Jesus. As Jesus tells the disciple Thomas, "If ye had known me, ye should have known my Father also: and from henceforth ye know him, and have seen him" (v. 7). When Philip then asks to see the Father, Jesus replies, "Have I been so long time with you, and yet hast thou not known me, Philip? He that hath seen me hath seen the Father" (v. 9b).

Once more, Eliakim is a model. His relationship with his father Hilkiah, though a virtual footnote in Eliakim's biblical biography, foreshadows our association with the Messiah and the Messiah's Father. Just as we only know about Eliakim's father Hilkiah through Eliakim, we only know the Messiah's Father through the Messiah Jesus. There is no way to God the Father except through Jesus Christ the Son, who is one with the Father and who is God in the flesh. We know Eliakim's father Hilkiah through Eliakim his son. Similarly, we know God the Father through Jesus the Son.

Like Eliakim, we are called to be faithful in the positions that God gives us. Even more importantly, when we are faithfully acting as God commands us and are seeking him—when we are being faithful for the right reasons—we are imitating Christ. Ephesians 5:1 directs us to be "followers of God." The Greek word for "followers" in this verse is μιμηταί (*mimētai*). Literally meaning "imitators," the Greek word is related to the English term "mimic."

---

3. Powell, s.v. "Eliakim."

We should be mimicking Christ. Ephesians 5 continues, "And walk in love, as Christ also hath loved us, and hath given himself for us an offering and a sacrifice to God for a sweetsmelling savour" (v. 2). The chapter highlights the distinction between Christian behavior and worldly behavior. "For ye were sometimes darkness, but now are ye light in the Lord: walk as children of light" (v. 8). Our imitation of Christ extends to the positions we hold as well as to our speech, actions, and general lifestyle.

Holding the key of David, Jesus is the ultimate Steward. As we see in Jesus, a steward's duty is to be as faithful as possible with his charges, priority, and demeanor. First Corinthians states, "Moreover it is required in stewards, that a man be found faithful" (4:2). Faithfulness was a prominent feature of Eliakim's character. If he had not been proven trustworthy, Eliakim could not have been chosen to do the job that Shebna was about to lose. Conversely, by his conduct, Shebna forfeited his position. God was not unfairly taking it away. Shebna gave the post away. Eliakim rightfully received it.

Being a steward does not always entail having a position that looks powerful and influential. First Peter says, "As every man hath received the gift, even so minister the same one to another, as good stewards of the manifold grace of God" (4:10). Whatever place we hold in the eyes of the world, we should strive to do our best to honor the Lord with what we are given. In the parable of the talents in Matt 25, the good stewards are praised and rewarded for being faithful, not for being wealthy or worldly (vv. 21, 23). The Lord knows his servants and their hearts toward him. He notices and remembers every single act and thought that is intended for his glory. For example, Heb 6:10 reads, "For God is not unrighteous to forget your work and labour of love, which ye have shewed toward his name, in that ye have ministered to the saints, and do minister." Faithful service with a faithful heart matters more than the size of our task. Additionally, the more faithful we are in what seems to be little, the more faithfulness we demonstrate for what seems to be big. "He that is faithful in that which is least is faithful also in much: and he that is unjust in the least is unjust also in much" (Luke 16:10).

Faithfulness may also take the form of standing firm to the Bible and its consistent portrayal of Jesus Christ as Lord and Savior. We can practice good stewardship by believing the Word, teaching biblical doctrine, and refusing to distort truth. In 1 Cor 4, Paul writes, "Let a man so account of us, as of the ministers of Christ, and stewards of the mysteries of God" (v. 1). Believers are entrusted with the doctrines of Jesus as God in the flesh and as the only way to heaven. A crucial aspect of faithful stewardship for all Christians is learning what the Bible says about Jesus and holding to Scripture as it presents itself. Romans 16 speaks of the gospel and "preaching of Jesus Christ, according to the revelation of the mystery, which was kept secret since the world began, But now is manifest" (vv. 25b–26a). We are to ground ourselves in the truth of the Messiah and the mystery of salvation through God alone, now revealed in the face of Jesus Christ. Colossians 2 instructs,

> As ye have therefore received Christ Jesus the Lord, so walk ye in him: Rooted and built up in him, and stablished in the faith, as ye have been taught, abounding therein with thanksgiving. (vv. 6–7)

In 2 Corinthians 4, Paul writes,

> For God, who commanded the light to shine out of darkness, hath shined in our hearts, to give the light of the knowledge of the glory of God in the face of Jesus Christ. But we have this treasure in earthen vessels, that the excellency of the power may be of God, and not of us. (vv. 6–7)

What a rich inheritance we receive through Jesus' faithfulness toward us. It is Jesus' power, not ours, that is revealed in good stewardship. We are merely earthly vessels. To think that we will reign with Christ in his eternal kingdom! What a breathtaking promise, and one to be faithful with as humble keepers, speakers, and believers of truth. Being faithful stewards, we share in the amazing glory Jesus has as he holds the key of David. Other people are watching to see how we live our lives and reflect Jesus in our everyday actions. In that sense, our access to God the Father is both a privilege that we have and a key that we hold as stewards of the gospel (1 Cor 4:1). An honor and obligation, such stewardship requires an obedience similar to what the Lord notes in the approved Philadelphian church.

Reflection Questions:

1. What is the key of David?
2. What are some future promises we have in Jesus as the King who holds the key of David? (Hint: read Rev 21–22.)
3. What "keys" do you hold today as a steward of gifts, talents, or responsibilities that God has given you?

4. After God promised David's family an eternal kingdom in 2 Sam 7, David immediately responded with humility and praise. How does David's reaction in 2 Sam 7 demonstrate biblical stewardship in action? (Consider Jesus as our model in Phil 2.)

5. As a Christian, your role as a steward extends to your words as well as your works. Ephesians 4 describes healthy speech that glorifies God by "speaking the truth in love" (v. 15a) and edifying the hearers (v. 29). How can you put responsible stewardship into practice with your speech? In particular, how can you be a faithful steward as you talk to other people today? For instance, you might go out of your way to encourage someone, or if possible, to share your testimony; avoid unnecessary confrontation where you would usually give in to anger, silently counting to ten so that no resentful comments slip out; speak up on behalf of truth in a situation where you have the opportunity; or resolve not to repeat a coarse story or word.

6. When you think of Jesus as the keyholder of David's house, you might think of Christmas and Jesus' birth as David's descendant. What are other implications of Jesus as the Messiah who forever holds the key of David's house?

6

Opportunity, an Open-and-Shut Case

> And to the angel of the church in Philadelphia write; These things saith he that is holy, he that is true, he that hath the key of David, *he that openeth, and no man shutteth; and shutteth, and no man openeth.* —Rev 3:7[1]

SPEAKING TO THE PHILADELPHIANS, Jesus emphasizes that he is holy and true, and that he holds the key of David. He quotes from Isa 22 in saying that he possesses the key to David's household. As the Messiah, Jesus is David's most prophesied descendant. He is the King of kings! The Old and New Testaments both affirm his royalty.

Holding the key of David is a claim to messiahship, kingship, and stewardship, but it is also something more. The Messiah, King, and Steward of God's household controls who can come and go. In John 10, Jesus alludes to his authority. He oversees all access into the heavenly kingdom: "I am the door: by me if any man enter in, he shall be saved, and shall go in and out, and find pasture" (v. 9). Revelation 3 speaks of the same authority and control. Jesus says that he "hath the key of David" and is the One "that openeth, and no man shutteth; and shutteth, and no man openeth" (Rev 3:7b).

These final lines of Christ's self-identification in the opening of the Philadelphian letter take us back to the Old Testament. There, reading the rest of the quote from Isa 22, we discover more context for Jesus' statement. Eliakim, the approved steward set to replace Hezekiah's unfaithful

---

1. Italics added.

servant Shebna, was appointed to receive the authority over the king's house. In Isa 22, the Lord says, "And the key of house of David will I lay upon his shoulder; so he shall open, and none shall shut; and he shall shut, and none shall open" (v. 22).

As the steward of the royal house, Eliakim would hold the keys to the kingdom. In that sense, he was a "door." His word carried weight. The access and opportunity supervised by the steward were reasons that the king needed such a trusted person to hold the position. The metaphorical doors controlled by the steward had to do with the inner workings of the kingdom.

When Jesus looks back to Isa 22, he is talking metaphorically about the keys of the kingdom of David as well as the keys to the heavenly kingdom. He is the most important door, just as he is the most important keyholder. In Rev 1, we are told that Christ even holds "the keys of hell and of death" (Rev 1:18b). The short version of the story is that Jesus controls it all. In other words, every opportunity that we receive, all of the access we have into the presence of the Lord God, comes through God the Son, Jesus Christ, "in whom we have boldness and access with confidence by the faith of him" (Eph 3:12).

Reflecting on these ideas of authority and access, we should stop to ask another question: What doors matter most to God? Western society has numerous time-worn adages about the Lord opening and shutting doors. One of the most popular sayings is "When God shuts a door, he opens a window." It's not uncommon to say that we're waiting on God to open a door. Using these sayings, we don't mean that we're sitting passively in a room until the Lord physically throws wide the door and beckons us out. At least, most of us don't mean that! Instead, when we say that we are waiting on the Lord to open a door, we typically mean that we are waiting on him to provide an opportunity, to guide us through a certain situation, to direct our steps where he'd like us to go. Doors, we implicitly understand, are symbols of access and entry. Doors lead us from one place to another. In the case of Jesus as the Door, we are being led from the kingdom of darkness into the kingdom of heaven (Col 1:13). Stepping through the Door takes us from one realm into another.

The Bible plainly states that Jesus is the door of salvation. As the only way to the Father, he is the only way to heaven, where we will experience eternal life in God's presence (John 10:1–16). The stakes could not be higher than eternal life or death. The door of salvation is the most important door ever, which is why it is so critical that we share the good news of who Jesus is. We need to point the way to Jesus in every aspect of our lives, sharing the gospel even when we are silent. Our actions can speak volumes.

The metaphor of the door should help us understand evangelism differently than we often do. In accepting Jesus as Lord and Savior, we are making an active choice to pass through him as the Door. We can indeed steer others toward Jesus, but it's up to them to choose whether or not they go through the Door. A vital place to apply this truth is with children who are raised attending church. Even though our kids may grow up going to church, they do not automatically become Christians because they belong to a churchgoing family. Walking through the physical door of a physical cathedral does nothing to secure eternal salvation, although entering the church may lead you to the altar where you will meet Jesus and finally walk through the real Door. Evangelism shows where and who the Door is. If we strip away the fact that each person must make an individual choice to pursue Jesus, or if we treat it like anyone is automatically saved, then we are neglecting the existence of the Door. Concealing or neglecting the truth of Christ is like leaving someone in a dark room and refusing to reveal where the only door is.

Even then, another hard truth of evangelism is that *recognizing* the door is not enough to make someone be saved. Someone can know where the door to the next room is without deciding to walk through that door. You can know who Jesus is and refuse to enter through him into salvation. In order to be saved, you must take the next step of going through the door. Once you know that Jesus is the Door, you have to come to him as your personal Lord and Savior, confessing your sins and asking for his forgiveness. The Lord enters into your heart as you enter into his family. The astounding truth that God actually dwells in our hearts is indispensable to remember when we share the gospel. To enter the next room, you must walk through the door that leads to that other room. To enter into heaven, you must walk through Jesus the Door that leads to forgiveness and new life.

In the end, our job as Christians is to tell others about who Jesus is, what he does, and why he came. Our listeners must choose how to respond to that knowledge. The choice to embrace or reject Jesus is an entirely personal one, involving an individual relationship between each person and God alone. In terms of evangelism and sharing the Door, what matters to God is that we are faithful stewards in how we live, act, and speak. Let Jesus be visible in our conduct and audible in our speech.

Let others see him in us, and let them be drawn to the door so that they can walk through it. They have to decide for themselves that they believe it is worth seeking and following Jesus, rather than just knowing who he is (Heb 11:6). The high calling of stewardship and evangelism cannot rely on us but must rely on Christ in us.

You can admire the finest, most splendid doorway from a distance or from mere inches away. You can stroke the exquisite carvings or woodwork of the threshold; you can run your fingers across the doorknob or the contours of the doorframe. Sincere as all of that admiration may be, it will never cause you to materialize on the other side of the door. That's the way it is with Jesus Christ, too. We can point to the door; that is our task, once we've walked through it. But we cannot compel others to come with us. They can stand outside the door and handle its edges or play with the doorknob. They can admire the door's shape or the fashion of the wood. None of that admiration takes someone into the next room. Admiring Jesus from a distance and calling him a "good man" or a "nice prophet" are simply not the same as entering through the Door of salvation by calling upon Jesus as Lord and Savior. God cares about our entry through the Door of Christ. He is not impressed by soliloquies on the Door's handiwork or by any other commendations from a distance.

Jesus promises the Philadelphians an open door. Since they are already saved, what door are these Christians being offered? They have passed through the door of salvation. They know Jesus Christ personally. What is this other door, and what import does it have for the Philadelphians' relationship with Jesus?

The answer is uniquely, even humorously, Philadelphian. If we've missed it elsewhere in our interactions with the Bible, God has a penchant for wordplay, puns, and clever connections. Chapter 2's survey of the seven Revelation churches barely scratches the surface of examples found in the other letters. The letter to Philadelphia is no exception. For the city of Philadelphia, connections are key (pun intended). One of the most fundamental traits of Philadelphia is that the ancient city enjoyed a location associated with gateways, doors, and connections. Philadelphia was a gateway city between the East and West. It was intended to be a place of access between cultures and peoples. Philadelphia itself was a type of door. Jesus is placing before the Christians an open door in a city that is associated with being an open door. He is making a pun, even as he is making a promise.

As a renowned gateway, an open door, and a place of opportunities, Philadelphia was the perfect site for missions work. Its advantages reflect exactly the sort of people the Philadelphians strove to be: missionaries in their everyday lives. As Philadelphian Christians, we can take our cue from our brothers and sisters of the first century. What ought we to be? What ought we to do? The Bible urges us to realize that God opens and shuts opportunities for his glory. He provides opportunities that bring him the greatest glory by bringing as many people to him as possible. The Lord is in the business of souls. As his servants and his Church, we are as well. Yes, every single detail of our lives is important to the Lord. We should pray about every single thing. In doing, so, however, we come to realize that there are no coincidences, no accidents, no doors that open without some reason. Every single thing has to do with the business of the gospel, every single thing has to do with the truth of who Jesus is, and every single thing has to do with his holiness.

In essence, every single thing in life comes down to what we make of the Door, Jesus Christ. Missions work in itself is not about building nice buildings or digging wells or handing out clothing. Those are all wonderful works and worthy causes, and they should be done. Nonetheless, these good deeds of missions are a means of living out the love we have for Christ and others. They themselves are not the goals of missions work. The goal of missions is telling others who Jesus is, so that they may find salvation in him. Christian missions work exists to spread spiritual health and wholeness through Christ. In the Great Commission, a quintessential statement of Christian purpose, Jesus instructs the disciples regarding missions:

> Go ye therefore, and teach all nations, baptizing them in the name of the Father, and of the Son, and of the Holy Ghost: Teaching them to observe all things whatsoever I have commanded you: and, lo, I am with you always, even unto the end of the world. Amen. (Matt 28:19–20)

Philadelphian Christians act on the principle set forth by Jesus. Wherever they are, these Christians are going for Christ. Whatever they do, they want to be living for Christ. They are a testimony on display for him. To be Philadelphian Christians, we should strive to mimic that kind of lifestyle, living it out by following Jesus for his glory.

Philadelphians are "goers" whether or not they are physically "on the go." The Philadelphian Christians addressed by Jesus lived in the city. They were there to receive his letter. They lived daily lives, like we do. They had jobs and families. They had homes, businesses, farms. They had cares and concerns. They ate, drank, and slept. They were people, just like us. They were being sent and were going, right where they were.

Some Philadelphians were physical goers, true. Some of them traveled to share the gospel. Perhaps many of them did. Others stayed in the region of Philadelphia and supported missions work by sending resources or teaching about Jesus through their words, lives, and actions. But all of them were on the move spiritually. All of them were missionaries. Even when they were at rest, these Christians were traveling closer to their final destination, living out a journey in the way they lived their lives. We are doing the same thing today. Some of us may be literal missionaries, traveling teachers, or itinerant preachers. Others of us may be stay-at-home entrepreneurs, homemakers, or close-to-home breadwinners.

The fact is that everyone, everywhere, is always bearing witness to something. Whether Christian or not, everyone is carrying a message related to some kind of ideology and belief system. Each person has some kind of expectation about the world's operations and its future; each person believes something. As Christians, our worldview is based on biblical evidence as well as on personal experiences. With Christ as our foundation, our witness ought never to be our own. All of us can watch for opportunities to honor Jesus by being honest, aspiring to have a clear conscience before God, and being unashamed of the truth of Scripture.

All of us are missionaries. The etymology of the word "missionary" speaks of someone who is "sent." God sends his Church to be his hands and feet in the world. Wherever we are and whatever we do, we are his Church right here and right now. Just such an awareness of being Christ's Body in every regard is a primary component of the church of Philadelphia. Philadelphians are always watching the doors that the Lord opens and shuts. As they pay attention to what he is doing, they attempt to put his workings in a wider eternal context by understanding that everything is to be done for God's glory. Everything is an opportunity. Closed doors are an opportunity to praise the Lord and trust him as we are faithful where we are right now. Open doors are an opportunity to walk into another career, location, group, or more, being faithful wherever we will be on the other side of the door.

The New Testament bears out this spirit of opportunity in every circumstance. Throughout the New Testament, the open door is a symbol for missions and opportunities to reach others for Christ. In Acts 14, the Jews of the early church celebrate the news that the Lord is making salvation available to gentiles. They're delighted to hear how God has "opened the door of faith unto the Gentiles" (v. 27b). In 1 Cor 16, Paul speaks of a "great" and "effectual" door that is being opened unto him in Ephesus, where he has wonderful opportunities to preach the Word (v. 9). In 2 Cor 2, Paul talks about how the Lord has given a door to preach (v. 12).

In Col 4, Paul asks the other believers to pray "that God would open unto us a door of utterance, to speak the mystery of Christ" (v. 3b). Paul is not specifically requesting to be released from prison. He is asking for the ability to share the gospel effectively and willingly—"as I ought to speak," he says (v. 4b). Paul's first and foremost concern was sharing the good news about Jesus. Praying for the opportunities and capabilities to share Jesus, the apostle was praying to be in accordance with the Lord's will. Paul got the message, in more ways than one. God cares about every detail in our lives. Every detail matters. And every detail, as Paul recognized, is about open or shut doors that present the holiness and truth of Jesus Christ.

Living in a gateway city of missions, at the edges of the Roman Empire and the entryway to the East, the Philadelphians understood what it meant to think about doors. They were paying attention to opportunities big and small. As Christians today, we are even now living in a gateway city. The entire world, in a sense, is a city on the threshold: the world is like a city on the brink of eternity. This is the moment to point out the true Door to salvation. It's the time to be watching for opportunities to point to Jesus through the doors that the Lord opens and shuts. As Philadelphian Christians, we can take advantage of this moment and carry out missions big or small, knowing that everything is for God's glory and that souls are on the line.

Reflection Questions:

1. Why would Jesus choose the metaphor of a door for speaking to the church at Philadelphia? What did this church's location have to do with gateways and doors?

2. Think back to the time when you came to Christ and entered through the door of salvation. How does belonging to his kingdom mean that we should live differently from the world? (You might look at 1 Pet 2 and 2 Tim 2.)

3. Can you recall a circumstance when the Lord seemed to close a door or remove an opportunity that you desperately wanted, only to give you a greater blessing in the closed door?

4. What are some occasions when opened or closed doors in your life specifically brought you the chance to tell someone else about Jesus, whether or not you took the opportunity?

5. Read Col 3:1–17. According to these verses, what kinds of opportunities do you have for sharing Jesus Christ in your behavior or words today?

6. "Going" for Christ can involve singing praise or resting on his promises where you are today, right now. How can quiet time with the Lord improve your relationship with him as you go out into the world? (Hint: Ps 119 and Matt 5–6 speak to the heart behind a healthy, growing relationship.)

7

Weakness, Meekness, and Other Strengths

> I know thy works: behold, *I have set before thee an open door, and no man can shut it: for thou hast a little strength*, and hast kept my word, and hast not denied my name. —Rev 3:8[1]

JESUS HAS NOW CONCLUDED the introduction of his letter to the Philadelphians. He identifies himself especially as he is known to this faithful church, telling them who has sent the letter to them. They can be assured that their mail comes from the highest source possible. Jesus is God, unchanging, holy, and true, and he is the Messiah born to David's line. He provides opportunities and has the final say on which doors open and which doors shut. It's as if Jesus has physically embossed the letterhead. His self-identification verifies that he is the sender. The book of Revelation comprises certified mail from God.

In the substance of the Philadelphian letter, Jesus shifts from identifying himself to making overt promises to the church. "I know thy works," he says. *I know all about you.* "Behold, I have set before thee an open door, and no man can shut it" (Rev 3:8b). If the Philadelphians wanted assurance, they have it in this statement. Jesus has more missions for them to accomplish. He has an open door ready, designed just for them. He's been listening and watching, and they can believe that he has plans in store for them.

1. Italics added.

What a joy for us to remember today. God has plans for his people. He has missions and outreach. He has lessons and blessings. Whatever twists and turns lie ahead in the road, whatever ruts or potholes, whatever valleys or hills, God sees them. Having the keys and the doors, he holds all of the control. Nothing slips by him. "The Lord shall preserve thy going out and thy coming in from this time forth, and even for evermore" (Ps 121:8). Suffering and heartache have a purpose. Happiness and celebration have a purpose. Yes—*everything* with God has purpose.

But what if you don't feel ready for the opportunity that God is sending you right now? What if the Lord is opening a door that frightens you, and you're terrified at what will happen next? Listen to what Jesus says: "I have set before thee an open door, and no man can shut it: for thou hast a little strength, and hast kept my word, and hast not denied my name" (Rev 3:8b). The Greek word "for" in this verse is an explanatory word. It can also be translated as "because" or "since" you have a little strength. The Lord is making a guarantee. This door is a good gift, granted under his protection and by his foresight. *Because I know you. I know what strength you do and don't have. I've been watching, and I care.* Don't worry, God says. This door fits what I know is just right for you at just the right time in just the right place.

The Philadelphians may have heaved a sigh of relief in hearing Christ speak these words to them. They only had to remain faithful to do their best with what they were given to do. He was ensuring a door that matched the strength they had. It wasn't that their task would suddenly become easy, but that they had Christ's reassurance and blessing to meet that task.

As we see in this exchange between Jesus and his beloved church, strength is not the same in God's eyes as it is in the world's eyes. The Philadelphians had to rely fully on Jesus. They knew that their dependency on Christ underpinned his entire relationship with them. The same lesson of reliance applies just as much for us today. We must depend on Jesus as the source of all of the strength that we have as Christians. As Paul famously writes in Phil 4:13, "I can do all things through Christ which strengtheneth me." The Greek text of Phil 4:13 refers to putting power into somebody. Whatever ability we have comes directly from Jesus, who supplies our strength and power.

First and Second Corinthians both contain other well-known descriptions of the Lord as our strength and power. In 1 Corinthians, Paul reminds the Christians in Corinth that their faith rests on Jesus Christ and the gospel of the cross. Even though the message of the cross looks like weakness and foolishness to the people of the world, it is actually the epitome of triumph. In his wisdom and strength, the Lord designs and provides atonement for our sins. "Because the foolishness of God is wiser than men; and the weakness of God is stronger than men," Paul proclaims (1:25).

Paul notes that God always prefers to work through those whom the world regards as weak and foolish. One of the Lord's primary purposes is to prove that the strength and wisdom of the world count as nothing to him. He chooses the weak, infirm, and lesser to demonstrate his glory so that "no flesh should glory in his presence" (1:29). Later in the same passage of 1 Cor 1, Paul quotes from Jer 9. The full passage he cites has a context much like that of 1 Corinthians.

> Thus saith the LORD, Let not the wise man glory in his wisdom, neither let the mighty man glory in his might, let not the rich man glory in his riches: But let him that glorieth glory in this, that he understandeth and knoweth me, that I am the LORD which exercise lovingkindness, judgment, and righteousness, in the earth: for in these things I delight, saith the Lord. (Jer 9:23–24)

Wisdom, might, and riches are imposing features on a worldly resume. They seem to open doors, secure opportunities, and pave a way forward in the world. For all of their earthly glory, however, when tied to worldly advancement, none of these things are impressive in the Lord's eyes. They cannot secure us a place in heaven or bring riches that accompany us after death. The only source of boasting we can ever truly have is found in our relationship to Jesus Christ. What carries weight in God's eyes is that we know and fear him. He delights in sharing his goodness with us; we can delight in finding our glory expressly in him.

Every time we declare "hallelujah" or its Latin counterpart *alleluia*, we are finding our strength in the Lord. The etymology for hallelujah rests on two words. The first is the Hebrew *hallel*, "praise." The second is "*Yah*" or "*Jah*," which is a short form of the Lord's holy Name Yahweh. "Praise" is related to a word root that has to do with clarity and brilliance. The root is associated with something that is worthy of celebration and commendation. An object of praise is something or someone worth boasting about in its own right. Thus, each time we say hallelujah, we are putting our boast in God. We are bragging on the Lord for who he is. Saying hallelujah is a way of professing "My boast is in the Lord!" or even "Glory to God!" This is the essence of our praise: recognizing that the Lord is worthy of celebration and renown, singing of his brilliance, and making a show of God for himself.[2]

The praise inherent in the word "hallelujah" is a brilliant reminder of the need to put God and not ourselves at the center of our boasts. Hallelujah is a glorification. Nevertheless, it's not a glorification of ourselves. The phrase is "praise to the Lord." The last half of the word is God's Name. The first half of the word directs glory and adoration to the Lord by his Name. Proper boasting and proper glory belong to the Lord.

Second Corinthians has more to say about glorying in the Lord and not ourselves. In chapter 12, Paul boasts on all that the Lord has done in him personally. The apostle declares that he could go on boasting, but that God has stopped him short. Although Paul has been given numerous visions and revelations, the Lord does not grant him free rein to gloat about them. Paul did not receive any insights, education, or opportunities for his own glory. Rather than permitting Paul to stumble into self-exaltation, God lovingly, knowingly allows something to interfere and to prevent the man from becoming carried away by himself. As Paul puts it, "There was given to me a thorn in the flesh, the messenger of Satan to buffet me, lest I should be exalted above measure" (12:7b).

Three times, Paul begged God to take away the infirmity that had been permitted to plague him (12:8). The Lord's answer addresses strength and weakness, putting all of human glory in its rightful place.

> And he said unto me, My grace is sufficient for thee: for my strength is made perfect in weakness. Most gladly therefore will I rather glory in my infirmities, that the power of Christ may rest upon me. Therefore I take pleasure in infirmities, in reproaches, in necessities, in persecutions, in distresses for Christ's sake: for when I am weak, then am I strong. (12:9–10)

Paul's declaration has merit for the Philadelphian church. The weakness of the Philadelphians is their strength. They have a little bit of strength left, Christ notes—only a little bit. But if they're committed to Jesus, what they have is always enough. Here lies the great paradox of strength. Real strength is found in emptying ourselves and embracing the process of being filled with the Lord and his Word. Paul passionately alludes to the removal of himself as he speaks of his life as an offering about to be completed (2 Tim 4:6, Phil 2:17). He was pouring himself out, conscious that the outpouring provided more space for the Lord to work. The more we are poured out

---

2. For more, see Strong, s.v. "halal."

for Christ, the more Christ pours into us. At our lowest points, in the most impossible moments, God's power shines the brightest.

While the Philadelphians only had a little strength, they were a church selected and set apart for big missions. Their weakness, through reliance on Christ alone, turned out to be the true source of their strength. We easily misunderstand strength and weakness, because we do not see ourselves the way that heaven does. It must have helped the Philadelphians when Jesus introduced himself as the source of holiness and truth. He gives them a lens for viewing themselves, but that lens is necessarily through him and who he is.

The best example of strength in the display of weakness is Jesus himself. As the Son of God, one with the Father, Jesus "made himself of no reputation" and came in human form (Phil 2:7a). He became a servant, humbling himself on our behalf, and took the lowly path to the cross. This is utter emptying of strength. Jesus' outpouring was done for a distinct purpose and with a loving heart.

In spite of his humility, Jesus had all strength available to him. As he affirms multiple times before the crucifixion, he has more than enough power to conquer every enemy. He lays down his life willingly, stating, "I have power to lay it down, and I have power to take it again" (John 10:18b). When Peter attempts to defend Jesus in the garden of Gethsemane, Jesus stops him. "Thinkest thou that I cannot now pray to my Father, and he shall presently give me more than twelve legions of angels?" (Matt 26:53). Nothing about the crucifixion represents any helplessness on Jesus' part. To the contrary, Jesus' death was not a tragedy, but a triumph, and an epic one at that.

In his willingness to suffer and die, Jesus demonstrates strength, tempered by discipline. He has complete assurance of the Father's will. His ability to keep himself and his power under perfect control is linked to his knowledge that he is doing what must be done. Hence, when Jesus halts Peter in the garden of Gethsemane, the Lord orders his disciple to sheathe the sword and asks, "The cup which my Father hath given me, shall I not drink it?" (John 18:11b).

Imitating the model of Christ, Philadelphian Christianity has to exhibit the same mindset. These imitators of Jesus are mimicking his voluntary sacrifice in life and, if necessary, in death. In Rev 3:7, the Lord says that he is holy, true, has the key of David, and opens and shuts doors. The Christians in Philadelphia must accept that. Jesus knows that they do accept it. Their acceptance is why he now places another open door before them. Being the legitimate King and Steward, Jesus can be trusted to grant opportunities and abilities when and where they're needed. If they live in faith and are faithful with what they have, the Philadelphians can rest in that assurance and push forward as he leads. They only need to be obedient to follow.

Obedience to follow is not weakness. It's the strength of humility and a proper awareness of place. It requires more willpower to know that God has power and uses it in his will for his glory than it does to parade ourselves and try to act in our strength. In the need for such willpower, we find another word that can help us to understand the strength the Lord desires in us: meekness.

For many people, the idea of "meekness" undoubtedly evokes an image of "weakness." The mental picture for meekness often looks something like a helpless little lamb, young and vulnerable, struggling to keep up as it trots along behind its shepherd. The illustration of the lamb emphasizes frailty. Rarely do we envision meekness as something powerful—say, in the face of a lion keeping its tight-knit muscles under strict control, surveying its kingdom from a flat rock or preparing to pounce upon its prey.

In our modern world, at least, we frequently tend to think of meekness as weakness, just as we typically picture strength in connection with muscles, impressive physical capabilities, and feats of brute force. Yet meekness is more about an attitude than an ability. The Greek word "meek" is πρᾶος (*praos*). Linguistically, this word has to do with a friendly, loving disposition.[3] Someone with meekness is mild and gentle because of the state of the heart, not the body.

As a church, the Philadelphians represented fraternal affection. Their very name "Philadelphia," meaning "brotherly love," suited a loving, friendly disposition that, based on the Revelation letter, they genuinely possessed. Philadelphia was a meek church in word and works. First John 3:23 sums it up nicely: "And this is his commandment, That we should believe on the name of his Son Jesus Christ, and love one another, as he gave us commandment." We already appreciate that these churchgoers were the real deal. They believed in Jesus as who God said he was, or else they would not have accepted him as being holy, true, or the Messiah. Their strength was borne out in the humble display of their meekness: it was a deliberate weakness that came about through their utter dependence on Christ. Like Paul, they were pouring themselves out in love for Jesus and

---

3. Cf. Liddell et al. (hereafter LSJ), *A Greek–English Lexicon*, s.v. "πρᾶος (III)."

for others, as verified and vindicated by the blessing of the open door that Christ conferred on them. The new open door was a gift that honored their weakness, promised the necessary strength, and encouraged them to continue living meekly in his sight.

Meekness in biblical terms is strength under disciplined control, such as we observe in Jesus Christ. Meekness is power tamed by knowledge and an awareness of proper place in relation to the Lord's sovereignty. Meekness is Jesus in all of his fullness accepting the cross and not fighting the necessity of death on the cross for us. Similarly, meekness is the Philadelphians' willingness to accept what must be and to pour out their strength in order for others to know Jesus. This is the meekness of Paul comparing himself to a drink offering being poured out for the Lord and for the sake of the gospel.

How do we foster hearts that focus on the Lord's strength through our weakness, developing habits of meekness and disciplined strength? Colossians 3 says,

> If ye then be risen with Christ, seek those things which are above, where Christ sitteth on the right hand of God. Set your affection on things above, not on things on the earth. For ye are dead, and your life is hid with Christ in God. (vv. 1–3)

Finding meekness is a lifelong pattern of pursuing meaning in Christ. In essence, living a Philadelphian life entails looking to Jesus and realizing that the world has a topsy-turvy view of morals and truth. Our real concerns should be with eternity and investing in what comes next. "When Christ, who is our life, shall appear, then shall ye also appear with him in glory" (Col 3:4). An intense, overriding focus on Christ and eternity will determine everything else in life for us. As Christians, we are meant to be living out a love letter to Jesus. As Jesus opens the Rev 3 letter with himself and his awesome qualities, we ought to open our letter with the same focus on him and his beauty. He is the letterhead on the paper of our lives. Or as Paul encourages us in Phil 3,

> I press toward the mark for the prize of the high calling of God in Christ Jesus. Let us therefore, as many as be perfect, be thus minded. (vv. 14–15a)

As we discipline ourselves and strive to put God's will front and center, better and more abundant fruits will emerge in our lives. Chief among those fruits is charity. It's "the bond of perfection" Paul writes (Col 3:14b).

Nineteenth-century Bible commentator G. H. Pember speaks of the love between Philadelphian Christians. He explains it as a love that is a side effect of our love for Jesus. For the Christian, mutual love is an irresistible result of our commitment to Christ. It transcends shared opinions or personal admiration. As Pember puts it, "It is a yearning toward all true believers . . . because they are the objects of Christ's affection."[4] Brotherly love is not worldly affection or simply liking others who have a mindset similar to ours. Biblically, brotherly love is the love shared by Christians as we recognize each other as members of the Church. Loving the Head of the Church, we cannot help but love the Church as the Body. The love we have for Jesus softens our hearts toward each other and will result in the weakness he desires in us. In our weakness, he can use us more than we can imagine.

Reflection Questions:

1. How does the world define and imagine strength? What is a primary difference between the world's view of strength and God's view of strength?

2. Read Matt 5 and consider the character traits in the Beatitudes (vv. 2–11). Does the world associate strength with these qualities?

3. Review the apostle Paul's backstory in Acts 8:1–3 and 9:1–30, Gal 1, and 2 Cor 12:1–11. Even though Paul was zealous first as an unbeliever and then later as a believer, how did the source of his strength change when he was saved?

4. Think back to the Beatitudes in Matt 5. What focus does someone with these traits have? How do these character qualities engage with meekness?

5. Christianity offers the ultimate paradox of emptying ourselves to be filled with Christ. Looking back on your life, what are some occasions when you saw God move at the times you felt most lost or confused?

6. Read 1 Cor 13, known as the "love chapter." Select one verse from this chapter and treat it as a challenge that you can take to God. What is a trait of love that you would like to see more of in your own life? How can you incorporate this trait into your prayer requests and your intentional habits?

---

4. Pember, *Great Prophecies*, 337.

8

Keeping the Word, Keeping the Faith

> I know thy works: behold, I have set before thee an open door, and no man can shut it: *for thou* hast a little strength, and *hast kept my word*, and hast not denied my name. —Rev 3:8[1]

In Rev 3:8, Jesus gives another reason for providing the Philadelphians with the opportunity to testify of him: "[Thou] hast kept my word." His statement is another commendation for the church. Because they have kept his word, Jesus will entrust them with even more. Being faithful stewards, they've established that they can manage the additional trust. After all, sharing the gospel is a privilege, and the Philadelphians are doing what they should be by sharing the gospel truth through their words and actions.

The ancient Philadelphians are not the only ones to receive the commandment to keep the Lord's word. God gives us the same instruction. If we're going to mimic the approved faith of the Philadelphians, then we must look more closely at what is involved with keeping Jesus' word. Throughout Scripture, it's a constant command. In John 14:15, Jesus says, "If ye love me, keep my commandments." First John reads,

> And he is the propitiation for our sins: and not for ours only, but also for the sins of the whole world. And hereby we do know that we know him, if we keep his commandments. He that saith, I know

---

1. Italics added.

him, and keepeth not his commandments, is a liar, and the truth is not in him. But whoso keepeth his word, in him verily is the love of God perfected: hereby know we that we are in him. (2:2–5)

Likewise, in John 15, the Lord declares, "If ye keep my commandments, ye shall abide in my love; even as I have kept my Father's commandments, and abide in his love" (v. 10). What is the Lord's commandment? Jesus articulates it clearly: "This is my commandment, That ye love one another, as I have loved you" (v. 12). To keep the Lord's word, we must love each other with Christian brotherly love.

Christian love for one another is quite the high calling. We cannot begin to follow Christ's commandment without having the proper starting point and motivation. Loving others is a step that comes after another step. The first step marks a crucial change of heart. Jesus' response to a scribe in Mark 12 helps us learn more about what it looks like. Here, the scribe asks Jesus about the greatest commandment in the law.

> And Jesus answered him, The first of all the commandments is, Hear, O Israel; The Lord our God is one Lord: And thou shalt love the Lord thy God with all thy heart, and with all thy soul, and with all thy mind, and with all thy strength: this is the first commandment. And the second is like, namely this, Thou shalt love thy neighbour as thyself. There is none other commandment greater than these. (vv. 29–31)

Love for God is the essence of the commandments (Matt 19:17). We keep the Lord's command to love one another by first loving the Lord himself. That is to say, we first love God, and because we love Christ, we will love others in the Body of Christ; and accordingly, because we love Christ and are part of the Body of Christ, we will love others outside of the Body by showing them the love of Christ. Keeping Jesus' word must start with continuously committing ourselves to loving the Lord with all that we are and have.

Moreover, keeping the Lord's command once more begins with putting your faith in Jesus. You cannot love God the Father without believing in Jesus Christ as the Son of God, one with the Father:

> And this is his commandment, That we should believe on the name of his Son Jesus Christ, and love one another, as he gave us commandment. And he that keepeth his commandments dwelleth in him, and he in him. And hereby we know that he abideth in us, by the Spirit which he hath given us. (1 John 3:23–24)

As Jesus puts it, "This is the work of God, that ye believe on him whom he hath sent" (John 6:29b). The entire keeping of God's work is bound up into one commandment: if you believe in God, then you must believe in Jesus, because he's the only way to the Father (John 14:6). To believe in Jesus requires humble submission. Admitting your own unholiness, you must acknowledge him as the only One who is perfect, holy, true, and pure. You lay down your life and ask him to take it. As a result, you are made new, and you can grow in love with him more and more. The growth of such love is both emotional and intellectual. Keeping his word is a whole-hearted commitment to trust and faith in Christ. It involves devotion of heart, mind, soul, and strength. Small wonder that becoming a Christian starts with realizing that we are imperfect and need Christ to transform us. Otherwise, how could we as sinners ever hope to have pure, complete love for anyone?

In Luke 8, Jesus describes a devoted heart: "An honest and good heart, having heard the word," keeps the word and "bring[s] forth fruit with patience" (v. 15b). A committed heart clings to the truth of what God says. We must engage with the Word of God on its own terms, taking its content in its context. Reading Scripture constantly and holding fast to it are essential components of our spiritual heart-health. "Hold fast that which is good," 1 Thessalonians admonishes. "Abstain from all appearance of evil" (5:21b–22).

The soul, or ψυχή (*psychē*) in the Greek, is sometimes translated as "life" (for example, as in Matt 2:20, 6:25, or 10:39). The *psychē* is a person's essence of life. It is his consciousness, personality, and self.[2] When Mary rejoices in the Lord's promise to her regarding the conception of Jesus, she praises the Lord, exclaiming, "My soul [ψυχή, *psychē*] doth magnify the Lord" (Luke 1:46b). Mary deliberately puts the essence of who she is as a person into praising the Lord. Purposefully magnifying God as greater than herself, Mary proclaims his glory: "For he that is mighty hath done to me great things; and holy is his name" (Luke 1:49). To devote our lives to the Lord, we must similarly commit our personality and conscious decisions to thinking about him and his works. The outpouring of self only comes with an inpouring of the Spirit.

The word translated as "mind" in the King James Version is διάνοια (*dianoia*), which can also be rendered as "thought," "intelligence," and "intention."[3] This word indicates intellectual purpose. It entails the capacities

2. Cf. LSJ, *A Greek–English Lexicon*, s.v. "ψυχή."
3. Cf. LSJ, *A Greek–English Lexicon*, s.v. "διάνοια."

for reasoning and logic. In 1 Pet 1, as Peter reminds believers of the promises and prophecies disclosed by God across the generations, the disciple encourages intelligent, intentional fixation on truth. Peter says, "Wherefore gird up the loins of your mind [διάνοια], be sober, and hope to the end for the grace that is to be brought unto you at the revelation of Jesus Christ" (1:13). Armed with the knowledge of God's assurances as a bedrock of faith, we are built up by meditating on his guarantees from the past. What the Lord has done and proven in earlier ages serves as a foundation for us in the present. Our faith increases as we apply our intelligence to recognizing fulfilled prophecies, remembering previous wonders, and focusing on the faithfulness of God. Through these practices and others like them, we exercise faith with our minds and not only with our emotions.

First Peter hints at another underlying characteristic that we will see again in the church of Philadelphia. Philadelphian Christianity reflects on the past, rests on the promises, and looks forward to the imminent coming of Christ. Philadelphian Christianity looks back *and* ahead—not only to the distant future of heaven with Jesus but also to the coming-any-second, it-could-be-right-now, imminent return of Jesus. Philadelphian Christianity keeps your mind on the Christ and your eye on the clouds. It fully expects that he could appear at any moment.

Philadelphian Christianity ties together expectation and energy. In Mark 12:30, when Jesus speaks of loving the Lord with all our heart, soul, mind, and strength, the Greek word for strength is ἰσχύς (*ischus*), translated as "strength," "power," or "might." Generally, ἰσχύς is a robust application of force that engages, withstands, resists, prevails. In a literary context, ἰσχύς can refer to vigor; in a military setting, to a general's main contingent of troops.[4] Jesus speaks of our power and might. While energy and ability certainly do not define our relationship with him or secure spiritual strength in his view, they are intended to be given over to the Lord. All of our power and determination should be oriented toward Christ first and foremost. As John the Baptist proclaims, "He must increase, but I must decrease" (John 3:30). Citing Jer 9, 1 Cor 1 reinforces the sentiment: "He that glorieth, let him glory in the Lord" (1 Cor 1:31b).

The best analogy for strength, force, and application of energy may be Paul's reference to Christianity as a physical contest. "Know ye not that they which run in a race run all, but one receiveth the prize? So run, that

---

4. Cf. LSJ, *A Greek–English Lexicon*, s.v. "ἰσχύς." For other occurrences in Scripture, see Strong, s.vv. "ischus," "ischuó"; for further explanation, see Thayer, s.v. "ἰσχύς."

ye may obtain" (1 Cor 9:24). Paul speaks of subjecting his body. In Phil 3, he again characterizes the Christian life as a contest: "I press toward the mark for the prize of the high calling of God in Christ Jesus" (v. 14). Our abilities, like every other part of us, should be invested in following the Lord. Investments take many forms, but they all focus on Jesus. Examples of eternal investment include reading the Bible, studying and internalizing its contents, making efforts to support evangelism, resisting worldly temptations and lusts, and living out our faith by imitating Christ and obeying his commands for daily life.

Ultimately, keeping the command of God is a whole-hearted, single-minded way of living. It's not that we do it as well as we should. Far from it. It's that we strive to do it intentionally and consistently. When, not if, we make mistakes, we have to give them to Christ and do our best to keep his commands again . . . and again . . . and again.

Signifying where our allegiance lies, the resolve to keep God's Word is a determining factor in our lives. Either we commit to Christ or to the world. There is no room for "both/and." Revelation 12 brings this critical and eternal "either/or" distinction to the fore. When the devil (Satan, the ancient serpent or dragon) is cast out of heaven, he makes war against the people of God. These saints are described as those who "keep the commandments of God, and have the testimony of Jesus Christ" (v. 17b). They serve as a stark contrast against the devotees of Satan. Because of their commitment to the Lord, Satan targets them with an unmatched ferocity and hatred. The devil's desperate goal is to derail the gospel. In his defiance against God and all that represents God's goodness, Satan most fiercely targets those who do serve God and keep God's commands.

Keeping God's command is something that the Philadelphians, the Christians of brotherly love, were doing well. They loved Jesus, so they loved the Church, so they acted in love by telling the world about him. Their words and works were a living testimony to the Savior. They were engaged in honoring, observing, and practicing what Christ said, not merely in letting his words go in one spiritual ear and out the other.

It cannot be emphasized enough that the Philadelphians were not legalists. They did not invest in good deeds with any expectation to be saved through performing those deeds. They understood that traditions, heritage, and works do not result in a person's salvation. First Corinthians 7 says, "Circumcision is nothing, and uncircumcision is nothing, but the keeping of the commandments of God" (v. 19). Ephesians 2 states:

> For by grace are ye saved through faith; and that not of yourselves: it is the gift of God: Not of works, lest any man should boast. For we are his workmanship, created in Christ Jesus unto good works, which God hath before ordained that we should walk in them. (vv. 8–10)

These verses apply quite well to the Christians of Philadelphia. Jesus had already introduced himself as the basis for their holiness. They knew better than to suppose that they were making their own way to heaven. We are reconciled to God through Jesus Christ alone (2 Cor 5:18). "For he is our peace," Eph 2 assures us (v. 14a).

Since we are reconciled to God through Christ, we now have peace with God and are made spiritually whole. Our faith is expressed in our works and priorities. "For the eyes of the Lord run to and fro throughout the whole earth, to shew himself strong in the behalf of them whose heart is perfect toward him" (2 Chr 16:9a). The word translated as "perfect" in this verse means "at peace with" or "complete toward" God.[5] With the same Hebrew root as the word *shalom*, it refers to "peace," "completeness," and "wholeness." Upon becoming Christians, we enter into a covenant of peace and friendship by finding fullness in Jesus Christ. Our lifestyle should reflect that covenant as we actively engage in following the Lord and doing what pleases him.

The word for "keep" in Rev 3:8 spotlights the healthy believer's active pursuit of God. "[Thou] hast kept my word," says the Lord. The Greek for "have kept" in this verse is ἐτήρησάς (*etērēsas*). A form of τηρέω (*tēreō*), the word ἐτήρησάς is an active verb. The Philadelphians are doing the action, not just watching it happen. A different form of the same word is found in 1 Cor 7:19, a verse that reiterates how our "keeping of the commandments of God" is what is important to him. The word "keeping" is τήρησις in the Greek (*tērēsis*). Closely related to τηρέω, it again emphasizes the Christian's purposeful, intentional loyalty toward God.

The Greek word *tēreō* indicates vigilance and attention. The term can also be rendered as "guard," "observe," or "protect."[6] We might colloquially translate τηρέω as "to keep a close eye on" or "to keep a tight rein on" something. The Philadelphian Christians are being described as people who pay attention to what Jesus said, when he said it, and how. Their eyes were unswervingly trained on truth. They must have been like the Berean believers

---

5. For more, see Strong, s.v. "shalem."
6. Cf. LSJ, *A Greek-English Lexicon*, s.v. "τηρέω."

commended in Acts 17 and celebrated for their rigorous attention to the Word of God. The Bereans "received the word with all readiness of mind, and searched the scriptures daily, whether those things were so" (v. 11b).

What is the outcome of strict, diligent searching of the Scriptures, and of paying attention to what Jesus said and applying it in every regard? Acts 17:12a gives us a beautiful demonstration: "Therefore many of them believed." In applying their minds, the Bereans found a place to apply their hearts. In applying their hearts, they discovered the truest, most fruitful application of their vigor and intellect.

Keeping Jesus' word and doing what we can to practice it will reap rewards, if we have the right motivation and a willing heart. The Bereans kept the Word in their hearts by constantly returning to the Bible. They searched the Scriptures for the Lord's commands. Seeing who Jesus is according to the Bible, witnessing how he has proven himself, and proclaiming him as the Lord and Savior, we, too, enjoy the benefits of a wonderful harvest in our hearts. If we receive what Jesus says and keep it in context, our faith will grow. Because the Bereans kept God's Word, when they first heard about Jesus and went to the Bible to evaluate the apostles' claims about him, they believed in Jesus. They recognized truth by its fruits.

"You've kept My word," Jesus tells the Philadelphian Christians. May that be said of us. May we be a Philadelphian remnant observing his teachings and pondering his words, treasuring them in our hearts and meditating on them every moment!

Reflection Questions:

1. If you're a Christian, God somehow and in some way opened the door for the gospel to reach you. Looking back, can you recall an opportunity that someone else took to share the good news of Jesus with you in a unique way?

2. Humility requires us to bow down to God with all that we are. Name one area of pride in your life and pray this area over to God today. What situations tend to provoke this pride in you? How can you avoid or identify them in your everyday life?

3. Physically, a healthy heart is fostered by a healthy diet and a healthy lifestyle. Spiritually, a healthy heart requires the same loving care. How does reading the Bible encourage a healthier spiritual heart?

KEEPING THE WORD, KEEPING THE FAITH

4. Read Phil 4:8 and compare its "diet" for a healthy heart and soul with what the world offers in the media, whether fiction or non-fiction, visual or audio. If you are striving to change your diet and to keep the Lord's Word, what unhealthy spiritual "food" can you cut out? Can you name one habit, behavior, or "guilty pleasure" that you know you need to remove from your life?

5. Paul compares the Christian life to a contest and marathon. Both of these physical feats involve training and alertness on an athlete's part. How or why do you think it would change your life to regard today as part of your training for eternity?

6. Acts 17:11 describes a Berean mindset of testing all claims against Scripture. Practice the Berean mindset today by thinking of something you heard or saw today that you know is not in alignment with what the Bible has to say. Make a list of three Scriptures that show how and why that view or opinion was wrong. (For this step, you might want to get a Bible concordance so that you can do a word search of the Word!)

9

In One Word, Salvation

> I know thy works: behold, I have set before thee an open door, and no man can shut it: *for thou* hast a little strength, and hast kept my word, and *hast not denied my name*. —Rev 3:8[1]

THE LORD NEXT COMMENDS the Philadelphians' steadfast commitment to him in another way. He has already shown his approval of them. They have a little strength remaining, meaning that they still cling to him personally with whatever dynamism and vigor they have left. They have kept his word, indicating that they hold to biblical doctrine with all that they have in them. Now, Jesus adds, "[Thou] hast not denied my name" (Rev 3:8).

Matthew 10 provides further context for this commendation. In Matt 10, Jesus is warning the disciples about persecution to come. They should expect afflictions. Yet while they can expect attacks from Satan and the world, believers are reminded that the only One really worth fearing is God himself. "And fear not them which kill the body, but are not able to kill the soul: but rather fear him which is able to destroy both soul and body in hell" (Matt 10:28). Persecution on earth can terrify and physically destroy, but it cannot undo the truth of who God is. All of the attacks in the world cannot do away with the truth of hell and the reality of punishment for sins. Our brothers and sisters who are constantly persecuted for Christian faith the world over continue to bear witness to this fact today. Each day, untold numbers of believers quietly choose martyrdom and face

---

1. Italics added.

death, knowing that eternity eclipses this temporary world. Those of us in the West would do well to learn from our fellow Christians' willingness to sacrifice everything for Jesus, especially in light of end-times prophecies about worldwide apostasy and persecution.

In the context of Matt 10, Jesus assures believers that standing fast to the end and fearing God alone will result in eternal peace for the soul. We must choose to accept or reject Christ on Earth, expecting that our decision here will have eternal effects.

> Whosoever therefore shall confess me before men, him will I confess also before my Father which is in heaven. But whosoever shall deny me before men, him will I also deny before my Father which is in heaven. (vv. 32–33)

Similarly, in 2 Tim 2:12b, we read that "if we deny him, he also will deny us." *If* we deny him, the verse reads. Denying Jesus is not the same as having weak faith or making mistakes. If Christians have weak faith and are not the perfect people we want to be, God knows our weakness: "If we believe not, yet he abideth faithful: he cannot deny himself" (2 Tim 2:13). Weak faith in Jesus is not the same as denying Jesus. Denying Christ includes rejecting him for who he is and refusing to believe that he is worth following.

It's not God's character that is on trial when we must choose between denying him or not. It's ours. We might fall down on the job when it comes to being holy. Obviously, as fallen humans, we will fall short when we rely on our own power. But if we belong to him and are trying to keep his commands, if we are endeavoring to love him with all that we are, God will not drop us or accidentally let go of us (John 10:28–29). Our connection to him comes down to the state of our hearts.

Romans 1 eloquently describes what it looks like to deny Jesus. The chapter traces the history of human rebellion and apostasy against God. According to Rom 1, creation testifies to the existence of God (v. 20). However, as the passage affirms, not everyone wants to choose to follow God, even if they know of him by name. Having seen testimonies of who God is, those who openly reject the Lord rob him of glory. "Because that, when they knew God, they glorified him not as God, neither were thankful; but became vain in their imaginations, and their foolish heart was darkened" (v. 21).

Romans goes on to say that these apostates foolishly turn away from God. Their rejection of God is a willful choice. It is a conscious decision to choose something or someone besides God. As active rebellion, apostasy is a self-deceptive choice to embrace evil and to worship the creature rather than the Creator (1:25).

The picture of apostasy in Rom 1 progresses. Circumstances grow worse. The people who reject the testimony of creation are declaring that they would prefer to worship virtually anything and anyone other than the true God. They choose sin and self-condemnation. Romans 1:28 explains, "And even as they did not like to retain God in their knowledge, God gave them over to a reprobate mind, to do those things which are not convenient." The KJV translation "convenient" in this verse renders the Greek word καθήκοντα (*kathēkonta*), which has the meaning of what is one's proper duty, or what is fitting and proper. God gives those who reject him over to themselves and to undesirable consequences because they refuse to do what is fitting. That is, the Lord delivers these rebels to their own lusts, allowing them to do things that are improper and not suited to his design for them. The people depicted in the passage overstep boundaries by embracing conduct that is naturally wrong, inappropriate, and unacceptable. The Lord will tolerate such evil for only a certain time.

Romans 1 is an illustration of denying God in practice. Rebels against the Lord reject his name and his power. Preferring evil, they commit wickedness and approve of its effects: "Who knowing the judgment of God, that they which commit such things are worthy of death, not only do the same, but have pleasure in them that do them" (v. 32).

In deciding to reject the Lord, the apostates of Rom 1 are following in the footsteps of Eve when she committed the first sin. The serpent tempted Eve by telling her that she and Adam would "be as gods, knowing good and evil" (Gen 3:5b). The people from Rom 1 are falling prey to the same self-deceptions as Eve did. They act on the assertion that they can either know good and evil as well as God does or that they can shape their own path, doing without God's standards. In every regard, they claim to know better than God and not to need the Lord as the only way to heaven.

In denying the need for God's standards, and thus in denying him as the Creator worthy of the only worship, these rebels are rejecting the one road to salvation. They are claiming that there is some other course besides what the Lord has provided. Here, they are actually denying who Jesus is. Trying to condemn God, they end up condemning themselves.

Returning to Revelation and the Philadelphians, we see that Jesus specifically says that the Christians of Philadelphia have not denied his name. They plainly are not the rebels of Rom 1. But in terms of a positive or negative response, what does Jesus' name mean? The angel Gabriel proclaims Jesus' name to both Mary and Joseph before Jesus is born. To Mary, the angel proclaims, "[Thou shalt] bring forth a son, and shalt call his name JESUS" (Luke 1:31b); to Joseph, "Thou shalt call his name JESUS: for he shall save his people from their sins" (Matt 1:21b). God was confirming Jesus' name for Mary and Joseph. Christ's name was linked to what he would do and be.

The name Jesus is the Greek word for the name Joshua. Joshua, in turn, is the English form of the Hebrew name Yeshua. Yeshua is the name assigned to the Messiah long before the angel Gabriel's first-century proclamations to Mary and Joseph. In Zech 6, back in the sixth century BC, God commands the prophet Zechariah to crown the current high priest Joshua as priest and king. "Behold the man whose name is The BRANCH" (Zech 6:12b), says the Lord. "The Branch" is a messianic title in other prophecies (Isa 4:2, 11:1; Jer 23:5, 33:15). God was using Zechariah to show that the Messiah, the Branch, would bear the same name as Joshua, the high priest in Zechariah's time. The Lord was sending a message to Zechariah, Joshua, and their contemporaries, as well as to those like us who would read Zechariah's words many centuries later. The Messiah was to be named Joshua. In Hebrew, the name Joshua is the same as the Hebrew name Yeshua and, in turn, as the Greek name Jesus. Zechariah was sent to crown the priest Joshua in order to symbolize that the Messiah, Yeshua, would be both high priest and King.

The name Yeshua is significant for other reasons besides fulfilling the prophecy given to Zechariah. Once we see what the name means, we gain a deeper understanding of how the Rom 1 apostasy willfully denies that Jesus is the only way to heaven. Yeshua means "salvation" or "God saves."[2] When we cry out to Jesus (Yeshua) and call upon him as our Lord and Savior, we are invoking him as our salvation. We are literally crying out "God saves!" The name "Jesus" means "salvation," and Jesus is salvation. As Peter announces in Acts 4, "Neither is there salvation in any other: for there is none other name under heaven given among men, whereby we must be saved" (v. 12).

To deny Jesus' name is to deny the truth of salvation through God alone. Those who deny Jesus Christ are denying the need to be saved through him as their Savior. They are denying that Jesus is, in fact, salvation.

---

2. Hershey, "Yeshua"; "No One Else," para. 13; and "Controversy over the Name," para. 14.

As we observe in Rom 1, denying God's path to salvation is declaring that you think you can invent your own standards and outcomes.

Being far more than a feel-good concept, temporary freedom, or fleeting state of mind, salvation is not meant to be fire insurance with a no-money-down guarantee. Etymologically, the word "salvation" traces back to the ancient word root *$solh_2$-.[3] This word root means "whole" and "sound." Salvation is the state of becoming whole and sound before God. Whereas sin corrupts us and takes us as its slaves (Rom 8:21, 2 Pet 2:19, Gal 6:8), salvation redeems us and makes us free. Salvation makes us whole in the eyes of God, enabling us to live with him forever as his glad, humble servants.

If we could successfully reject God and instead choose to worship creatures and creation, then we would not need to worship the Creator as the Bible commands. In effect, we would be replacing him. Such a "replacement" mentality is exactly what we witness in Satan's creed, as recorded in Isa 14. Satan, the devil, was once a holy, heavenly being. Yet he fell into proud, sinful love of self. His manifesto proclaims, "I will ascend into heaven, I will exalt my throne above the stars of God. . . . I will ascend above the heights of the clouds; I will be like the most High" (vv. 13b–14). Although, on a broader scale, Satan's mindset is what we observe in Rom 1. The devil is making the same brazen declaration that the Rom 1 apostates are. If we could worship ourselves and succeed, then we would not need God. If Satan could worship himself and succeed in imposing his standards of right and wrong, then he would not be subject to God.

The satanic philosophy of Isa 14 and Rom 1 might sound desirable. It may even seem feasible, except it so happens that we *do* need God. Despite our feelings and fleshly lusts, God does exist and cannot be erased. Even the demons realize God's permanency. James 2 notes that they "also believe, and tremble" (v. 19b). The demons are aware that the Lord is everlasting. To them, his unchanging reality is a source of undying terror. Demons tremble at the name of Jesus because they understand that he truly is God.

Furthermore, even Satan's manifesto betrays his unhappy recognition that God is the Most High. Notice the precise wording in Isa 14: Satan wants to be *like* God, but Satan does not say that he's going to surpass the Lord. What does this mean? Is Satan being humble and stopping at the top? No; if there were something better than God, Satan would crave it. His declaration shows that he stops at the top because there is

---

3. Watkins, *American Heritage Dictionary*, s.v. "sol-."

nothing higher! The devil has experienced the throne room of the Lord. Thus, the devil understands that no one can be greater than God, and the devil's highest aspiration is to become *like* God. Knowing there's no higher anything or anybody, even though he hates the Lord with his entire being, Satan cannot imagine exceeding God. The devil himself cannot begin to conceive of anything or anybody greater than the one true God. Satan loathes God and truth, but the satanic creed tacitly confirms that there is nothing and nobody higher than Jesus, the King of kings.

Someday, everybody is going to realize the same truth of God's superiority. Everyone will know the supreme nature of the Lord as the Most High. Not only can no one surpass God, but as we see in Isa 14, no one can conjure up the remotest idea of something or someone higher than God. There is no way to go higher than the highest. Scripture is crystal clear. One day, we will all have to admit who Jesus is, whether we like it or not.

The universal recognition of Jesus as salvation does not suggest that everyone will be saved and go to heaven. Satan and his forces continue to try to overthrow the truth of Jesus' name. Demons and all who join Satan and reject God's sovereignty will take themselves to the very pit of hell in their insane attempts to replace the Lord (Rev 20:10–15).

Surrounded by the insanity of sin, however, it is a comfort for Christians to remember the unequivocal truth of salvation. God's grace is evident in the coming of Jesus Christ. His mercy endures forever because Jesus comes to be who he is. Because Jesus, whose name means "salvation," is salvation, we can freely experience salvation in him and find new life that will endure eternally.

> Wherefore God also hath highly exalted him, and given him a name which is above every name: That at the name of Jesus every knee should bow, of things in heaven, and things in earth, and things under the earth; And that every tongue should confess that Jesus Christ is Lord, to the glory of God the Father. (Phil 2:9–11)

Yes, God exists. Everyone will eventually have to admit that he does and that, in the flesh, he has come as Jesus Christ. Everybody is going to have to bow before Jesus and profess who he is.

Again, the sweeping confession of Jesus in Philippians does not insinuate that everybody is going to be saved. Hebrews 11 defines coming to God in faith as having two elements: "But without faith it is impossible to please him: for he that cometh to God must believe that he is, and that he is a rewarder of them that diligently seek him" (v. 6). One section of v. 6 looks to God's existence; the other, to God's worthiness.

The first part of Heb 11:6 has to do with the first part of coming to God in faith. Believing that God exists is critical to believing in him. Here, once more, we need to be extremely conscientious and read Scripture for what it says. There is a critical difference between (*a*) the universal confession of Jesus as Lord in Phil 2 and (*b*) a personal confession of Jesus as Lord now, during a person's own lifetime. Compare the picture of salvation in Rom 10:9: "That if thou shalt confess with thy mouth the Lord Jesus, and shalt believe in thine heart that God hath raised him from the dead, thou shalt be saved." The word for "confess" is ὁμολογήσῃς (*homologēsēs*), from ὁμολογέω (*homologeō*). The word refers to conceding, admitting, or generally agreeing upon a joint conclusion. The Greek in Phil 2 is a variation of the same word for "confess" as seen in Rom 10. In Phil 2, everyone has to admit (ἐξομολογήσηται, *exomologēsētai*) who Jesus is, because he is God (v. 11).

Like Phil 2, Rom 10:9 speaks of confessing Jesus as the Lord. The pivotal distinction between the two passages is when and how the confession happens. Phil 2 refers to the end of the ages, *after* the time for choosing salvation has ended. Isaiah 55:6 says, "Seek ye the LORD while he may be found, call ye upon him while he is near." The opportunity to come to Jesus as Lord and Savior and to be saved is a limited-time offer, only open for the short duration of a human life. You have your lifetime to make the decision; that's it. Not everyone will come to acknowledge the truth of Jesus during this limited lifetime.

Philippians 2 describes the period when all earthly lives have been lived and all decisions have been made once and for all. Ultimately, no one will be able to deny who Jesus is, in the sense that everyone will have to admit that Jesus is who he claims to be. Isaiah 45 confirms,

> Look unto me, and be ye saved, all the ends of the earth: for I am God, and there is none else. I have sworn by myself, the word is gone out of my mouth in righteousness, and shall not return, That unto me every knee shall bow, every tongue shall swear. (vv. 22–23; cf. Rom 14:11–12)

Christ has been magnified and will be openly recognized. Into eternity, Jesus cannot be ignored. Everyone will have to concede that God does exist; everyone will have to acknowledge the truth of biblical reality.

By contrast, the personal confession process of Rom 10 does not happen at the end of the ages. Rather, Rom 10 describes the age of grace in which we currently live. Right now, today, you can come to Jesus and find salvation in him. Knowing that he exists, you can come running to him now, when you can be saved. You can acknowledge he is real and act on it by stating that you believe he is the One he says he is. The gospel is "the word of faith" being preached today (Rom 10:8b).

Belief in Jesus as the only One worth calling upon for salvation is where the second part of Heb 11:6 comes into play. The second part of Heb 11:6 says that the one who comes to God must believe "that he is a rewarder of them that diligently seek him." You cannot simply believe that Jesus exists. There is more to it than knowing God is real: there is a personal relationship of reconciliation with him as the Lord.

Philippians 2 states that everyone in the end will have to believe that God exists, even as the devils do (Jas 2:19). That eventual admission, however grudgingly made, is not the same as being saved and receiving entry into eternal life. The saved soul deliberately chooses to accept Jesus in faith, affirming that yes, Christ not only exists, but is *worth following*. The person who comes to Jesus for forgiveness is deciding to turn away from the world and toward Christ, reckoning that the gains are greater than the losses. To become a Christian, you must deny that salvation is found anywhere other than in the name of Jesus, Yeshua.

As we know, it is the name of Jesus that brings salvation. Jesus is salvation in name and incarnate. When the Philadelphians refuse to deny Christ's name, they are living in faith as defined by Heb 11:6. They acknowledge that the God of the Bible exists and that he is worth following, exactly as the Bible says the Lord is. God richly rewards those who seek him, and his rewards are worth pursuing. As the Lord told Abraham early in their relationship: "I am thy shield, and thy exceeding great reward" (Gen 15:1b). Abraham believed and found righteousness through the Lord (Gen 15:6).

For us as fallen humans, how odd it is to realize that creation knows who its Lord really is, and desires to see him glorified. After all, we do not see trees quivering with excitement or hear stars whimpering in anticipation. We do not truly comprehend how devastating the curse of sin is, nor do we understand the gravity of Adam and Eve's choice or our own sinful choices when we look around us. But creation is waiting because creation is suffering. Sin inflicts suffering on the sinner and the sinner's surroundings.

Romans 1 shows this truth, describing the current situation as one in which people choose to do unnatural things with their bodies because they decide to reject the Lord for who he is. Their perversion of heart results in the perversion of their bodies. They bear the brunt of their sin. Everything else in creation waits in agony, desperately yearning for the day when the curse of sin will be lifted and when Jesus will be revealed and worshiped. Romans 8 says that "the whole creation groaneth and travaileth in pain together until now" (v. 22b). All of eternity is on the edge of its seat, aching for the Lord to be revealed in his glory, along with the people he has redeemed for himself (v. 19). All of creation is longing for the Philadelphian Christians to be manifest through God's glory! First John 3 says, "Beloved, now are we the sons of God, and it doth not yet appear what we shall be: but we know that, when he shall appear, we shall be like him; for we shall see him as he is" (v. 2).

Creation is waiting to see Yeshua proclaimed, crowned, and seated upon his throne. The Philadelphian Christians join in the anticipation. When they refuse to deny Christ by name, their eyes are trained on the bigger picture of eternity. They are looking past the world of today and into the world of tomorrow, glimpsing a new heavens and new earth where the Lord sits as salvation enthroned.

Denying the name of Jesus is the same as squeezing our eyes shut, plugging our spiritual ears, and pretending that creation does not scream the truth of Scripture. Calling upon the name of Jesus honors him and praises his sacrifice. God saves! Why? Because Yeshua—salvation—lives. Jesus lives!

Reflection Questions:

1. During his ministry, how was Jesus persecuted for rightly declaring that he is salvation?

2. Why do you think the world persecutes Christians today? Why do unbelievers care if someone believes in Jesus or not? (Read John 15.)

3. Romans 1 describes the choice between good and evil. According to the Bible, rebellion is a decision to put our self-made standards above God's objective, holy standards. How do you see this choice being made in the world around you right now?

4. Long before the Savior was born, God revealed that the Messiah's name would be Joshua/Yeshua, which is the name Jesus (Zech 6:11–13). How does this name point to the plan of salvation?

5. Why is it impossible to believe at the same time that (*a*) God is wrong about sin but (*b*) we need Jesus alone to save us from sin?

6. Hebrews 11 contains a long list of Old Testament saints, people who lived before Jesus was born but who died. Select two people from the list and consider how they lived in faith of future salvation provided through God alone.

10

The Church as the Church

> Behold, I will make them of the synagogue of Satan, which say they are Jews, and are not, but do lie; behold, I will make them to come and worship before thy feet, and to know that I have loved thee. —Rev 3:9

INSTEAD OF CONDEMNATION, THE Philadelphians receive only commendations from Christ. After promising them an open door for witnessing, the Lord makes a further commitment: "Behold, I will make them of the synagogue of Satan, which say they are Jews, and are not, but do lie; behold, I will make them to come and worship before thy feet, and to know that I have loved thee" (Rev 3:9).

The synagogue of Satan appears elsewhere in the book of Revelation. In chapter 2, speaking to the persecuted church of Smyrna, Jesus mentions the same group: "I know thy works, and tribulation, and poverty, (but thou art rich) and I know the blasphemy of them which say they are Jews, and are not, but are the synagogue of Satan" (v. 9). Since Smyrna is the only other church besides Philadelphia that has no negative associations and receives purely positive news, it's particularly significant that Jesus names the synagogue of Satan in the letter to Smyrna. The satanic adherents persecute both the Smyrnans and the Philadelphians. They especially attack the real Christians, but do not bother to expend the same kind of effort in assaulting the corrupt or dying churches. Satan is not wasting resources when and where he feels that he can achieve victory by other means.

The two letters' descriptions of the synagogue of Satan have common denominators. First, Christ refers to the people of this group as those who "say they are Jews, and are not" (2:9b, 3:9b). Second, the people of this group attack the Christians on the grounds of identity. Both groups are being used by Satan to harm the church as much as possible.

With the Smyrnans, Jesus assures believers that he recognizes the slander against the Christians. The unbelievers are not going unnoticed. Jesus sees how they are abusing his people. He will judge the unbelievers as blasphemers.

For the Philadelphians, the assurance is slightly different. Jesus tells the church of Philadelphia that they can expect the synagogue of Satan to admit the truth of who the Philadelphians are in Christ. The unbelievers mentioned in this letter will be caught out in their lie and will be forced to confess it. Revelation 3 leaves open the possibility that the unbelievers attacking the Philadelphians will even repent and express regret as they acknowledge that they were lying about who they themselves were and who the Philadelphians were not. They may be converted to Christianity. The letter to Smyrna does not say anything similar about unbelievers attacking the persecuted church of Smyrnans. The letter to Philadelphia hints that at least some of the unbelievers in this synagogue of Satan may have a positive outcome of salvation. Currently anti-Christians, they might come to know and embrace the truth of Christ.

To be absolutely clear, the Bible never promotes hatred of Jews or gentiles. We are called to care for all people and to speak God's truth in love. "Lean not unto thine own understanding" (Prov 3:5b). With that in mind, who are the assemblies coming against the church? Moving through time, they appear to fit two groups. The first group is that of ethnic Jews trying to dismiss Christian claims to God. They deny who Jesus is and call him a fraud. The second group is ethnic gentiles claiming to dismiss Israel's relationship to God. This group alleges that they have replaced Israel. They deny God's ongoing promises to Israel as a nation while redefining themselves.

Historically, the church of Smyrna adhered to its Jewish roots, but was reviled for it. The Christians of Smyrna celebrated Passover instead of Easter, for instance, and held relatively tightly to their apostolic beginnings, being more like the early church in their practices. However, because the Smyrnans believed in Jesus as the Messiah, unbelievers criticized the Smyrnan Christians for applying the significance of the Jewish feasts and law to Jesus Christ.

The unbelieving Jews are usually considered to have been a primary source of persecution against the believers at Smyrna. Eusebius and others record the hatred that non-Messianic Jews—that is, Jews who denied Jesus as the Christ—harbored for the Smyrnan Christians. Jesus condemns such unbelieving Jews as those who claimed to be believers in God but who in reality belonged to Satan. They attended services at the synagogue, exercising the law and proclaiming the prophets, but they were not committed to God in their hearts. In denouncing the Christians, they denounced the Christ. In Satan's service, they helped send Christian Jews and Christian gentiles to death.[1]

Certainly, the synagogue of Satan is not a title being applied to all Jews, and it is definitely not a validation for anti-Semitism in any form or at any time. These Jewish unbelievers were no better or worse than gentile unbelievers in the eyes of God. Jesus confronts other legalistic Jewish leaders for their service to Satan in the supposed name of God. He rebukes them for performing the lusts of their father, the devil (John 8:44a). But Jesus was a Jew. He loves Jews and is anything but anti-Semitic. Rather, he was exposing his antagonists' satanic and sinful hearts, a heart that lies beneath any rebellion against God, whether the rebel is a Jew or gentile.

The Smyrnan synagogue of Satan seems to have been comprised of people who assumed that they were closer to God because of their ethnicity. In their fervor, they persecuted Christians. It was unacceptable to them that any believer in Jesus should claim to know God. Still, their objection to Christianity is not all that unusual. Ethnicity is not the only obstacle some people argue stands between God and an individual heart. Cults frequently insist that you cannot know God unless you come through them first. Quite frankly, anyone who argues against salvation through faith in Christ alone is repeating the same old deception as the Revelation synagogues of Satan. The Bible consistently proclaims that God does not accept or require any mediator except Jesus Christ (Gal 3:13–29).

At Smyrna, the synagogue of Satan was attacking believers on the basis of identity. The believers identified as God's people through Christ. The unbelievers argued that the Christians could not be God's people, because

---

1. For more regarding pressure on the Smyrnan church, especially the non-Messianic Jews' contribution to persecution in Smyrna, see Treybig, "Smyrna" (also citing Eusebius's remarks in *Church History*, 5.24).

only the physical descendants of Abraham could enjoy special promises from the Lord. Conversely, Scripture explains that all believers in Christ receive the spiritual blessings promised to Abraham's descendants. Salvation extends to gentiles as well as to Jews, and only through the grace given us through Christ. "Therefore being justified by faith, we have peace with God through our Lord Jesus Christ" (Rom 5:1).

At Philadelphia, the synagogue of Satan is a similar group accusing Christians on the grounds of identity. Like the unbelievers at Smyrna, these antagonists claim to know God more closely. They challenge the church's connection to him. These opponents argued that God did not actually love the Philadelphians in the way that the Philadelphians said he did.[2] Jesus vows to set the record straight: "Behold, I will make them to come and worship before thy feet, and to know that I have loved thee" (Rev 3:9b). Yielding to the truth, these foes will someday admit who is who and what is what.

Jesus singles out both of these hostile groups as purveyors of bad doctrine. He also specifies that the synagogues of Satan in both cities are attacking God by attacking believers. In each case, the deceiving and self-deceived synagogue of Satan asserts that it has a higher knowledge of God, and assails God's people as not really belonging to him. The synagogue of Satan attacks good doctrine by attacking Israel as God's chosen nation and by attacking the Church as God's chosen Bride.

Essentially, the synagogue of Satan defies God by striving to set its own standards and lean on its own understanding. By contrast, Philadelphian Christianity rests on the truth of God's ongoing promises as the Lord has pronounced them. He makes promises to the Church as the Church. He makes promises to the nation of Israel as the nation of Israel. These promises are not yet all fulfilled, but they will be, because of who Jesus is. The Bible describes Israel and the Church as separate entities, clarifying that the Church contains saved Jews and saved gentiles alike. The satanic deceptions at work in Smyrna and Philadelphia argue otherwise. They deny that Christians can partake of spiritual blessings or that the Church can be loved by God. In both cities, these groups are worldly people who decry Christian identity in Christ, particularly where it concerns the unity of saved Jews and gentiles and the remarkable role of Israel.

---

2. Along those lines, in his letter to the Philadelphians, Ignatius urges the Christians there not to be converted to or affected by Judaism and Jewish legalism (*Letter to the Philadelphians*, 6).

Putting Philadelphia in context, the union of Jewish and gentile Christians in Christ is a distinctly fitting emphasis for this city. We are looking at a missionary church that advances the Church as a united Body of Christ centered on Christ. In Philadelphia the secular city, Eastern and Western cultures meet. They are merged to become a synthetic whole. Philadelphia is by definition a gateway city. In Philadelphia the church, two also become one. Here, the two are saved Jews and gentiles. They are both brought into the Church, God's Body, as God's redeemed.

Acts 10 recounts the original, official evangelism of gentiles. Jews rejoice to learn that God is giving the gentiles the opportunity to be saved and to receive the gift of the Holy Spirit. In Eph 2, Paul celebrates the unity of Jews and gentiles who come to Jesus and become one in him.

> But now in Christ Jesus ye who sometimes were far off are made nigh by the blood of Christ. For he is our peace, who hath made both one, and hath broken down the middle wall of partition between us; Having abolished in his flesh the enmity, even the law of commandments contained in ordinances; for to make in himself of twain one new man, so making peace; And that he might reconcile both unto God in one body by the cross, having slain the enmity thereby: And came and preached peace to you which were afar off, and to them that were nigh. (vv. 13–17)

In Christ, gentiles as well as Jews can be saved. "For there is no difference between the Jew and the Greek," Paul writes, referring to Jews and gentiles, "for the same Lord over all is rich unto all that call upon him" (Rom 10:12). Jews and gentiles join together as one in the Body of Christ.

The Revelation letters are not the only verses that respond to these attacks on biblical identities. Earlier in the first century, the book of Romans reacts to the same heretical views targeting Israel and the Church. Romans 9–11 confront several misconceptions about Israel and the Church. Paul spells out that the Jews remain God's chosen nation, despite their collective unbelief. Saved Jews are not rejecting their heritage, but are embracing it, because the Mosaic law and priesthood foreshadow the Messiah. Israel has not lost its identity through Christ. It will someday discover its true identity through him. At that time, following a national revival described in Zech 12, Hos 5:15, and other passages, the Jews will enjoy the fulfillment of remaining promises such as full regathering in the promised land, physical favor, and spiritual wholeness. Jesus Christ will one day reign from the city of Jerusalem.

Paul further affirms that the Church is a separate entity from Israel and that it does not replace or outdo Israel. The Church delights in its own blessings. One of its primary purposes is to motivate unbelieving Jews to seek God and discover a personal relationship with Jesus the Messiah. Paul quotes from the Lord's words to Israel in Deut 32:21b: "I will provoke you to jealousy by them that are no people" (Rom 10:19b). God was telling the Jews beforehand about gentiles who would join the Church by coming to faith in Christ. As evangelism continues in the age of grace, when we may come to Jesus freely, find salvation openly in him, and become part of the Church, Paul additionally warns saved gentiles not to become condescending toward unsaved Jews. Chapters 9 through 11 of Romans emphasize that both the Church and Israel are and remain part of God's bigger plans.

The same misconceptions about identities persist in the church institution across the generations. Many denominations and teachers, no doubt true believers among them, mistakenly teach that the Church has replaced Israel, that the Church will receive the promises declared to the Jewish people, that the Old Testament promises were only allegories or symbols, or that the modern state of Israel is an anomaly, unrelated to prophecy. A simplified label for some of these views is "replacement theology," a.k.a. "supersessionism," which takes Rom 9–11 out of context. Replacement theology incorrectly treats the Church as Israel. As we see from the Revelation letters, such ideas are dangerous and insidious. Paul addresses them handily. Speaking of the nation Israel, he asks, "Hath God cast away his people?" He then answers the question with a resounding negative: "God forbid" (Rom 11:1b). The Lord has not done away with Israel. He has formed for himself a separate Body called the Church, with members coming from among the Jews and the gentiles.

Instructed by the book of Romans and the Bible as a whole, Philadelphian Christianity diligently tests all doctrine against Scripture to see what God says about the past, present, and future for Israel and the Church. Their interactions with Christ define their worldview. Consequently, the Philadelphian church actively seeks to interpret all identities and ideologies through the lens of the Bible. Testifying to God's sovereignty, these Christians cling to Jesus and let God determine their roles. They trust and profess that the Lord knows what he is doing. Philadelphian Christians can experience the sweet relief expressed by Paul at the end of Rom 11:

> O the depth of the riches both of the wisdom and knowledge
> of God! how unsearchable are his judgments, and his ways past

finding out! For who hath known the mind of the Lord? or who hath been his counsellor? Or who hath first given to him, and it shall be recompensed unto him again? For of him, and through him, and to him, are all things: to whom be glory for ever. Amen. (vv. 33–36)

Practicing good stewardship always involves returning to Scripture and learning what the Bible says about personal identity either in Christ or apart from him. Scripture encourages believers to be faithful stewards of "the mysteries of God" (1 Cor 4:1b–2), urging Christians to hold to the teachings that God gives and to let God interpret everything for us. The Philadelphians are to do their job. Their work is to serve God, not to seek vengeance against their foes in the synagogue of Satan. The Lord will take care of the situation with their opponents.

The synagogue of Satan presents a collective attack on good doctrine and on the identity of God's people in multiple roles and places. Everywhere, as at Smyrna and Philadelphia, the pure doctrine of Jesus as the Head of the Church is still under constant attack. Philadelphia, uniquely, will witness many of its attackers humbly admit the truth, possibly ready to be saved and to grow in Jesus. At any rate, at both Smyrna and Philadelphia, we notice a constant theme. The Church's battle with the synagogue of Satan is one of continuous identity politics. Satan drives wedges wherever he can. He specializes in deception, confusion, and destruction. Our duty is to be vigilant and to engage in spiritual warfare by reading, studying, teaching, and clinging to Jesus. The Philadelphian Christian is called to "be strong in the Lord, and in the power of his might" (Eph 6:10b).

Many astonishingly gracious promises are reserved for God's people. Some promises are for the nation of Israel—others, for the Church, which includes saved Jews and saved gentiles. These promises, these gifts, underscore the absolute faithfulness of God, as well as the importance of our identity in Jesus. And so Jesus tells the Philadelphians: today's slanderers and blasphemers will soon come to know that I have loved you and that I am God. Anyone listening will hear, because "he that is of God heareth God's words" (John 8:47a).

Speaking of the Church, Eph 4 declares, "There is one body, and one Spirit" (v. 4a). God's people are defined by Jesus, by God alone. Christ is our Head (Eph 4:15). Jesus opened his letter to the Philadelphians by reminding them that he is holy and true. He identifies himself as the Head of the Church, and the Philadelphian Christians as the people of his Church.

Just as everyone will finally be forced to bow to him and acknowledge his name, so too will everyone have to admit that the people who hold to the truth of Christ and the Bible alone are God's own Church. The world does not have permission or prerogative to redefine the Church based on human standards or claims to truth. When Jesus is glorified, his people are glorified. Their belief in Jesus as the Son of God is vindicated. When they humble themselves and exalt him, they are exalted. The missionary church of brotherly love partakes of the promise that they will rejoice in the Savior's joy, no matter how much the synagogue of Satan rages against them and against their fellow believers in Smyrna.

Reflection Questions:

1. According to John 16:2, there will be and are people who kill Christians and claim to be doing it for God. How do we see this kind of persecution unfolding in the synagogues of Satan described in Rev 2–3?

2. Many people today maintain that the Church has replaced the Jews. Read Rom 9–11. What does Paul say about the relationship between and roles of Israel and the Church?

3. Read Gen 12:1–7 and 13:14–17. These verses offer a snapshot of God's promises to Abraham, Isaac, Jacob, and their descendants. Next, turn to Ezek 40–48. Based on these passages alone, what promises remain for the Jewish people as a nation? (Consider specific promises about monarchy in Jerusalem, celebration of the Jewish feasts, the future of Israel's priesthood, or the size and division of the land.)

4. Read 1 Pet 2:9–10. What eternal promises remain for all Christians today?

5. The word "synagogue" in the Greek means a type of assembly or coming together. Assemblies, conferences, and conventions happen around us all the time. Some have good principles; some do not. Why is it important to pay attention to what groups are doing as well as to what they publish in their statements of purpose/faith?

6. Exod 23:2a states, "Thou shalt not follow a multitude to do evil." How can peer pressure encourage people to embrace sin, especially when we are spending less time in Scripture?

11

Of Patience and Promises

Because thou hast kept the word of my patience, I also will keep thee from the hour of temptation, which shall come upon all the world, to try them that dwell upon the earth. —Rev 3:10[1]

PHILADELPHIA RECEIVES SEVERAL PRECIOUS promises linked to the church's faithfulness. The Philadelphians are given an opportunity that will not be taken away from them but one that is guaranteed by Jesus himself. Philadelphia's enemies will come to recognize that these Christians represent the true Body of Christ and are set apart by God as part of his Church. Now, because of the state of their hearts, the Christians of Philadelphia are assured a very unique type of protection. "Because thou hast kept the word of my patience, I also will keep thee from the hour of temptation, which shall come upon all the world, to try them that dwell upon the earth" (Rev 3:10).

"Because thou has kept the word of my patience," Jesus declares. Life has not been completely smooth for the Philadelphian church. We already know that they have a little strength, indicating that they have come under immense pressure. We know that the synagogue of Satan has been attacking them. The Philadelphians have faced and are facing opposition, although they hold fast in Christ. They are being proven under trial. Notably, the word for "temptation" in Rev 3:10 can also be translated as "trial" or "testing." Here, "testing" speaks of putting somebody

1. Italics added.

or something to the test, or making proof of that person or thing. Being tested and tried, the Philadelphians' weakness is an opportunity to manifest and prove God's strength.

As observed by biblical archaeologist William Ramsay, Jesus' promise of protection would have resounded well with the Philadelphians for another reason. Philadelphia was a site of pronounced earthquake activity. A particularly damaging quake had occurred in AD 17, almost eighty years prior to Christ's letter. The people of Philadelphia knew that living within the city walls could be dangerous. They were mindful that a sudden trial could happen any minute, coming upon them in the form of a devastating earthquake. Many Philadelphians chose to mitigate the threat by dwelling outside of the city. They lived as farmers, working the fertile soil and tending to their prosperous vineyards. To these wary Philadelphians, Christ's offer of deliverance is a sweet promise to be cherished. He will rescue them from an even worse trial that is about to come upon all of those who dwell on the earth.[2]

In spite of the trials they have faced both spiritually and physically, the Philadelphians press on in their faith. Be it persecution or earthquake, nothing hinders them from continuing in their labor for the Lord. They have kept God's word, showing that they have endeavored to love God and, as a result, to love one another and to speak the truth of the gospel. They have not denied Jesus' name. They ascribe power to the name of Jesus Christ. As witnessed in Jesus' words to them, the Philadelphians recognize that salvation is found in Jesus Christ alone. They understand that Jesus is God's Messiah and is one with God the Father.

Rev 3:8 says that the Philadelphians have kept and are keeping Jesus' word. In v. 10, the Greek phrasing is virtually the same as in v. 8. The Philadelphians have done their best to obey Jesus' instructions. They have endured. They are not fly-by-night or happy-go-lucky believers, nor are they in the church solely to obtain fire insurance. They are the sort of people whom Jesus compares to good soil in Luke 8: "They, which in an honest and good heart, having heard the word, keep it, and bring forth fruit with patience" (v. 15b).

We can compare this kind of soil and people with the other types represented in the same parable from Luke 8, a parable about seed (the Word of God) being sown in different types of soil (human hearts). Seed fallen on the road and trampled or eaten by birds symbolizes people who

---

2. See Ramsay, *Letters to the Seven Churches*, 396–98, 406–7.

never become saved. The devil plucks the Word out of these hearts. Rocky soil stands for people who have joy at hearing the Word, but never develop roots. When trials come, these hearts lose faith and slip away. Other seed falls into thorny patches and represents hearts that, though they hear the Word, "are choked with cares and riches and pleasures of this life" (Luke 8:14b). These hearts bear no fruit because they become so entangled by the world and its lusts.

Then there's the good soil, observed in the Philadelphian and Smyrnan hearts. Both of these churches must endure something. Smyrna must endure to the death; Philadelphia must endure in the missions field—and endure until an unexpected rescue. The good soil "bring[s] forth fruit with patience" (Luke 8:15b). Fruit is produced as the people of God act as the people of God, being uncompromising in their morals and conduct. Luke 8:16 says, "No man, when he hath lighted a candle, covereth it with a vessel, or putteth it under a bed; but setteth it on a candlestick, that they which enter in may see the light." Smyrna and Philadelphia are Christians letting their light shine. The light is Christ in them. As John declares, Jesus is the Light of the World (John 1:9).

The Greek word "patience" or "endurance" in Rev 3:10 is ὑπομονή (*hypomonē*). This word is sometimes translated as "perseverance." It literally speaks of "holding out" and having something left over. In Rom 8:25, we have patience (ὑπομονή, *hypomonē*) in hoping for what we do not see. Romans 15:4 assures us that "whatsoever things were written aforetime were written for our learning, that we through patience [ὑπομονή] and comfort of the scriptures might have hope" (Rom 15:4). The next verse describes God as the "God of patience [ὑπομονή] and consolation" (Rom 15:5b). Hebrews 10 states, "For ye have need of patience [ὑπομονή], that, after ye have done the will of God, ye might receive the promise" (v. 36); while Heb 12:1b urges us to "run with patience [ὑπομονή] the race that is set before us."

Lessons of perseverance, patience, and endurance are woven throughout the Bible.[3] "Behold, we count them happy which endure," James remarks (Jas 5:11a). The term he uses for those "which endure" is ὑπομείναντας (*hypomeinantas*), a word derived from the same root as ὑπομονή. James goes on: "Ye have heard the patience [ὑπομονή] of Job, and have seen the end of the Lord; that the Lord is very pitiful, and of tender mercy" (Jas 5:11b). The Lord blesses his people as they endure and wait

---

3. Strong, s.v. "hupomoné."

for his promises. His higher purpose is compassionate and merciful, so that suffering and patience will, in the end, reveal miraculously better, more desirable outcomes than we could have imagined.

The Philadelphians, being people of hope, are enduring while they wait for what they cannot see. They "walk by faith, not by sight" (2 Cor 5:7b). Even though they have not seen Jesus in the flesh, they believe, and are therefore blessed by Jesus himself (John 20:29).

Importantly for us, Philadelphian Christianity avidly looks for what we cannot see now, in our day. Titus 2 reads,

> For the grace of God that bringeth salvation hath appeared to all men, Teaching us that, denying ungodliness and worldly lusts, we should live soberly, righteously, and godly, in this present world; Looking for that blessed hope, and the glorious appearing of the great God and our Saviour Jesus Christ. (vv. 11–13)

We do not see Jesus at this moment, but we await the blessed hope of his glorious appearing. This hope is the comforting expectation that Jesus Christ might appear at any second to claim his Church, his Bride. Paul consoled the anxious Christians of Thessalonica with the assurance that Jesus is coming again to take his people to himself. In 1 Thessalonians, Paul gives one of the clearest accounts of this event of Jesus' coming to take his Bride. The event, called the Rapture, will occur at any time.

> For the Lord himself shall descend from heaven with a shout, with the voice of the archangel, and with the trump of God: and the dead in Christ shall rise first: Then we which are alive and remain shall be caught up together with them in the clouds, to meet the Lord in the air: and so shall we ever be with the Lord. Wherefore comfort one another with these words. (4:16–18)

Not all Christians will live to experience the sudden return of Jesus for the Church in the Rapture. Some Christians, like the Smyrnans, will suffer and not be alive at the time of the Rapture. Some Christians, like many others across the generations, will live and die normal lifespans, and will likewise not be alive on the earth at the time of the Rapture. Still, someday, a certain generation of believers will joyfully take part in the Rapture and be caught up to heaven with the Lord.

Happily enough, this comfort is found directly in the letter to the Philadelphians. Recall Rev 3:10: "Because thou has kept the word of my patience, I also will keep thee from the hour of temptation, which shall come upon all the world, to try them that dwell upon the earth." The word for "thou hast kept" in the first half of v. 10 is ἐτήρησας (*etērēsas*), which can be translated as "keep," "guard," "watch," or "observe." The same word is used in the second half of the verse: "[I] will keep," τηρήσω (*tērēsō*). The Philadelphians' love for Jesus shows itself in keeping his Word. They endeavor to uphold the Word of God as seen in God's written Word (the Bible) and in God's living Word (Jesus Christ, God in the flesh). The only way to keep the word is to keep the Word, Jesus Christ, in our hearts. Otherwise, we cannot begin to follow Jesus' commands or to treasure him.

In return for keeping his word, the Philadelphians are kept by Christ. Not only are they kept by Christ in that they are saved and have eternal life in Jesus, but the Philadelphian Christians additionally have Christ's word that they will be kept from the coming hour of judgment. Jesus speaks of literal judgment that will one day come upon the entire world. He never suggests that Smyrnan Christians have done anything wrong or are worth less than the Philadelphians, however. The difference between Smyrnans and Philadelphians has nothing to do with the quality of the believers or with some kind of vendetta for previous sins. Rather, the difference between the promises to the two churches indicates that the literal churches in the first century came to different outcomes and that God has different purposes in mind for each individual believer's life. In the development of the church, foreshadowed in the seven churches, the Philadelphians' assurance looks to a generation of Christians who will literally be removed from Earth before the world passes into the intense end-times judgments. We may or may not be alive when the Rapture occurs. Nonetheless, if you are a Christian alive at the time Jesus returns for his Bride in the Rapture, you are going straight to his side in the clouds!

While the seven churches absolutely reflect seven real-life churches in the first century, we also observe that the patterns of the letters suggest the historical development of the church as an institution. In other words, as discussed in the church overview in chapter 2, Ephesus corresponds to a real-life church, as well as to the era of the early church. This first era of the church is called the "apostolic age." The apostolic age was the age of the apostles and their direct involvement with the growth of the Church. Smyrna corresponds to the church as it entered into extreme persecution; Pergamon, to the historical period in which the church institution began to mingle with the world; and so on and so forth, with the church institution developing along the lines of the churches in Rev 2–3.

Advancing through time, the church of Philadelphia is a model for the missionary era. This period roughly correlates to the missionary efforts of the eighteenth, nineteenth, and early twentieth centuries AD, when modern evangelism was at a peak around the world. Bible translation, foreign missions aid, church planting, evangelism training, and ministry publications are among the hallmarks and activities of the missionary age. The missionary age is responsible for sowing seeds of Christianity across the globe, or at least for watering the seeds that were in some cases planted generations ago.

Following that line of thought, the church of Philadelphia is the remnant of the missionary-minded church today. This is the faithful church that continues into the last days, yet is removed before the judgment of the Lord, exactly as promised in God's words about the Rapture. The faithful believers have Jesus' pledge that they will be rescued from the most intense tribulation that the world has ever experienced.

Revelation 3 suggests that the Philadelphian Christians can expect to be removed before God unleashes global judgments upon those who dwell on Earth at that time. These worldwide judgments of the last seven years and especially the last three and a half years before Jesus' final return are most detailed in the book of Revelation. The seven-year period is commonly called the Tribulation; the last three and a half years of it, the Great Tribulation. (A better, more precise name for the seven years is the Seventieth Week of Daniel, a title drawn from the prophecies of Dan 9.) Earth-dwellers, the people who inhabit or dwell upon the Earth, is a name found throughout biblical prophecy, as in Rev 8:13, 11:10, 13:14, 17:8, or Isa 24:17 and 26:21, to name only a few examples. The title refers to the people who live on Earth through the Revelation judgments, but who continue to rebel against God.

The promise of rescue does not protect faithful believers from all trials and tribulations. Jesus says to expect troubles. "In the world ye shall have tribulation: but be of good cheer; I have overcome the world" (John 16:33b). First Peter admonishes believers to expect grievous persecutions: "Beloved, think it not strange concerning the fiery trial which is to try you, as though some strange thing happened unto you" (1 Pet 4:12). Tribulations are not strange or unanticipated. "All that will live godly in Christ Jesus shall suffer persecution," Paul tells Timothy (2 Tim 3:12b).

In the Beatitudes, Christ calls persecution a blessing on the true believer:

> Blessed are ye, when men shall revile you, and persecute you, and shall say all manner of evil against you falsely, for my sake. Rejoice, and be exceeding glad: for great is your reward in heaven: for so persecuted they the prophets which were before you. (Matt 5:11–12)

Jesus states that you are blessed *when* you are persecuted, not if. Knowing that his words are faithful and true, we can be sure that they have equal meaning for Philadelphian Christianity in any age. Those who are living out their faith can expect that the world will not approve. One of the harshest realities of the end times is that the world's disapproval will only become more ruthless as Earth's final days approach. Immediately after warning Timothy that all believers will suffer persecution, Paul adds that "evil men and seducers shall wax worse and worse, deceiving, and being deceived" (2 Tim 3:13b).

The Philadelphians contend with teachings of apostasy and other forms of rebellion against the Lord. Today, such defiance against God continues to be a major factor in society and in the world's rejection of the Lord. The trend of apostasy, or falling away, is becoming more prominent. It will culminate in one of the most hopeless institutional church situations of all: Laodicea, a nominal church that does what is right in its own eyes and forsakes truth. Second Timothy cautions believers against the coming apostasy.

> For the time will come when they will not endure sound doctrine; but after their own lusts shall they heap to themselves teachers, having itching ears; And they shall turn away their ears from the truth, and shall be turned unto fables. (4:3–4)

First Timothy 4 speaks of the same event of apostasy. "Now the Spirit speaketh expressly, that in the latter times some shall depart from the faith" (v. 1a).

The contrast between Philadelphia and the nominal "church" of Laodicea could not be stronger. Whereas the Philadelphians endure with what little strength they have, keep the Lord's word, and refuse to deny him, the Laodiceans disgust the Lord so much that he is about to "spue" them out of his mouth (Rev 3:16b). The Laodiceans believe that they are rich and do not need anything from the Lord (Rev 3:17). While the Philadelphians recognize their full dependence on Jesus Christ as Lord and Savior, the Laodiceans are too self-fulfilled to realize that they are "wretched, and miserable, and poor, and blind, and naked" (Rev 3:17b).

As Christians, we should be paying attention to everything in the Bible. Prophecies of the end times are all over Scripture. Biblical eschatology, the study of the end times, has to be based on these prophecies. Our sense of eschatology must involve an awareness of the apostasy and the Rapture, because both events are found in the Bible. Among other places, they're right here in Revelation. Any true but complacent believers who are in the church of Laodicea should expect to be rebuked and chastened (Rev 3:19).

Even earlier in Revelation, the church of Thyatira is warned about a coming time of horrendous tribulation. Thyatira is church number four of the seven. Thyatira is corrupted by adultery and idolatry with the world and its false religions. This institution stubbornly allows evil doctrine to persist in the church. According to Jesus, the people invested in the adultery and other deeds will be cast "into great tribulation" (Rev 2:22b). Thyatira was engaged in apostasy and the nominal Christianity that come to obvious fruition in Laodicea. For choosing to ally with the world and its ungodly doctrines, these adulterous, lost, and self-deceived churches are warned that they can expect to go through tribulation. The Lord speaks of the last years of the world before his coming, alerting us that these years will bring the worst tribulation ever seen by the human race:

> For then shall be great tribulation, such as was not since the beginning of the world to this time, no, nor ever shall be. And except those days should be shortened, there should no flesh be saved: but for the elect's sake those days shall be shortened. (Matt 24:21–22)

The searing reality of end-times events is patently obvious in the letters to the seven churches. Jesus' words to these apostate churches are grave. His promise to them is real: you will suffer, but if you are willing to be saved, you will be saved as through fire.

Meanwhile, Philadelphia's faithful believers have a promise just as real. If they hold fast to Jesus, they will be removed before the worst tribulation that is to come upon the earth. Unbelievers left behind by the Rapture will still be able to be saved, but will have to live through the period of tribulation. New believers will have to suffer faithfully to death or, as rare as it might be, to survive to the Second Coming of Jesus (Rev 19). These Christians, seen by John in Rev 7, are frequently called Tribulation saints.

Again, the promise in Rev 3 does not imply that the Philadelphians are saved from every trial and tribulation. Otherwise, why would they have only a little strength remaining by the time that Jesus sends his letter to them? Conversely, the promise reminds Christians today that (*a*) we should endeavor to be faithful through all trials; (*b*) we have a greater promise that should always encourage our hearts, because Christians living at the Rapture will go to be with Christ in an instant; and (*c*) we need to be evangelizing and sharing the truth of the gospel, spreading the blessed hope of Jesus Christ. Eternity is what matters today.

Reflection Questions:

1. Read the parable of the sower in Luke 8:4–15. If you've watched seeds sprout, you know that they require time, nutrition, and water. How is the growth process of plants an analogy for the seeds and good soil in the parable?
2. Why should Christians expect increasing persecution?
3. How does the endurance of the Philadelphian Christian reflect a long-term perspective? (A helpful passage for this question is Phil 3.)
4. How does a long-term perspective help motivate missions and evangelism? (Consider Phil 1.)
5. When you read the letters to Philadelphia and Laodicea in Rev 3, how do these letters demonstrate the different perspectives that these two churches have?
6. Many Christians are afraid to contemplate the end times. Name one thing the Bible tells us to expect in the last days. For your topic, you might think of apostasy (1 Tim 4), the Antichrist (Rev 13, 2 Thess 2), the Rapture (1 Thess 4), or prophecies in Dan 9, for example. As a Christian, how can studying this topic give you a greater hope in Christ?

12

Jesus, Coming Quickly

> Because thou hast kept the word of my patience, *I also will keep thee from the hour of temptation,* which shall come upon all the world, to try them that dwell upon the earth. —Rev 3:10[1]

As described in the previous chapter, Jesus' words to the Philadelphians provide Christians with wonderful, ongoing hope. We saw how Christ's promises remind Christians today that (*a*) we should endeavor to be faithful through all trials; (*b*) we have a greater promise that should always encourage our hearts, because Christians living at the time of the Rapture will be with Christ in an instant; and (*c*) we need to be evangelizing and sharing the truth of the gospel, spreading the blessed hope of Jesus Christ. "We shall not all sleep, but we shall all be changed" (1 Cor 15:51b).

Every Christian can expect deliverance into eternal life. The Philadelphian Christians include believers alive at the time when Jesus returns in the sky to claim his Bride, the Church. Only God knows who in the Church Invisible will be living on Earth to participate in the Rapture. Whatever the case, Philadelphian Christians can expect deliverance in the Rapture. Such anticipation is an amazing incentive to be watching for Jesus' return! "Watch therefore," Jesus states, "for ye know not what hour your Lord doth come" (Matt 24:42). He tells us to be ready: "For in such an hour as ye think not the Son of man cometh" (Matt 24:44b). The directive is so important

---

1. Italics added.

that he soon repeats it: "Watch therefore, for ye know neither the day nor the hour wherein the Son of man cometh" (Matt 25:13).

The Philadelphian church is a church that is told to remember and emphasize the doctrine of the imminency of Christ's coming—that is, the teaching that the Rapture could happen at any time. The imminency of Jesus' return for the Church can be an intimidating thought, in some regards. The looming Rapture highlights the fact that eternity is on our doorstep. As days pass and the time goes by, we tend not to think about eternity as something that could begin right now. Yet in the instant of the Rapture, a new phase begins for the Church. Christians will be swept away into heaven with Jesus.

Historically, the apostolic church was much more excited about the immediacy of Jesus' coming. Paul addressed 1 Thess 4 to Christians in the first century AD. These believers were living in such anticipation that they were concerned for Christians who had already died and thus had missed the Rapture event. Paul's original audience of the first century might have been quite shocked to learn that 1 Thessalonians, a letter to their church, would still be read by eager Christians two thousand years later.

The disciples were expecting Jesus' earthly kingdom even before the crucifixion. They hoped either that the First Coming would be Jesus' only coming and that he would stay to establish his reign immediately, or that the interlude between the First and Second Comings would be extremely short and that they would live to see Jesus return during their natural lifetimes. In response to their questions about the future, Jesus outlines Christian eschatology. His reply, recorded in Matt 24, is paralleled by numerous passages in Mark 13, Luke 17, and Luke 21. In Matt 24:3, the disciples begin asking anxious questions about what to expect. What does Jesus mean when talking about the Second Temple's destruction? What is the sign that he is coming? What is the sign of the end of this age? Even at that early time, before the birth of the Church, the disciples were watching and waiting in expectation. Could they expect the end to come soon?

Two millennia later, we're closer than ever to the fulfillment of the eschatological outline given by Jesus and other end-times prophecies throughout the Bible. Revelation 22 concludes with the affirmation of what Christ tells the disciples in Matt 24. "Surely I come quickly" (Rev 22:20b). By comparison with the believers of the first century, Christians living in the twenty-first century must be extraordinarily closer to Jesus' return. The Rapture could have come at any moment then, and it could certainly come at any moment now.

The most famous Rapture description in Scripture, Paul's words to the Thessalonian believers explain that the event of the Rapture unfolds in an instantaneous series of steps. Rapture is merely a form of the Latin word *rapiemur*, translating to the phrase "we will be caught up" or "snatched away" (1 Thess 4:17). "Rapture" refers to being "caught up" or "snatched away." The Rapture itself should not be confused with Christ's arrival on Earth in Rev 19. The Rev 19 event can be called the Revelation of Jesus. It is the fulfillment of the completed Second Coming of Christ. As detailed in other passages such as Matt 24:30, Zech 14, and Rev 1:7, everyone on Earth will see Jesus' return in Rev 19. By contrast, the Rapture occurs earlier and is more private. Only believers will see Jesus' return in 1 Thess 4, although the entire world will witness the sudden disappearance of the true Christians. How the world will interpret what has happened is another matter entirely. Sadly, it may be that the institutional church will be so corrupt that it will contain very few believers and that the church institution will not be much affected by the change.

Jesus states that the Rapture will take place at a completely unknown time and usher in a time of judgment on the world (Matt 24:37–42). First Thessalonians 5 characterizes the day of the Rapture as the believers' deliverance from God's wrath (v. 9). On that day, the Lord Jesus will "descend from heaven with a shout, with the voice of the archangel, and with the trump of God" (1 Thess 4:16b). These steps reflect the Jewish wedding ceremony, where the groom suddenly arrives for his bride. He lets out a shout as the attending procession relays his arrival and sounds the trumpet.

As noted by Arnold Fruchtenbaum, the steps of the Rapture also reflect a normal military structure: "First, the chief commander gives the shout; next, the sub-commander repeats the command of the chief commander; and then, the trumpeter sounds the specific note so that the soldiers will know exactly what the command is."[2] In the Rapture, the Lord gives a shout, like the commander-in-chief issuing his initial command; the archangel, in the role of his sub-commander, relays the order; and the trumpet sounds. "Hence, the trumpet sound will trigger the rapture itself," Fruchtenbaum writes. "This trumpet blast will serve as a summons for the action to begin."[3]

---

2. Fruchtenbaum, *Feasts and Fasts*, 166.
3. Fruchtenbaum, *Feasts and Fasts*, 166.

At the trumpet's call, the Church will be caught up to join the Lord, just as the bride goes to accompany her groom and as the army follows its general. The Church will ever after be with Christ. "Wherefore comfort one another with these words," Paul writes (1 Thess 4:18). Every member of the Church will be with Jesus from that day forth and will receive a new, glorified body. "In a moment, in the twinkling of an eye, at the last trump: for the trumpet shall sound, and the dead shall be raised incorruptible, and we shall be changed" (1 Cor 15:52).

With this beautiful, any-minute-now future in mind, we as the Church should be living with heightened excitement in spite of the growing darkness of the world. We can have an even greater expectation to see Jesus come for us anytime. Philadelphian Christians possessed a burning sense of anticipation. They lived in a state of joyful hope, staking their futures on Jesus. We need to exercise similar hope, infusing our lives with the expectation of Jesus. His return is a reality with ramifications for every moment of the day and night.

How can we foster a sense of eager anticipation for Jesus' return? Pember offers a solution drawn from Scripture: the study of prophecy. First, he notes, we are commanded to study prophecy, and when we are obedient to God's commands, the Lord gives grace. God acknowledges and strengthens his own people, promising them eternal hope. Revelation 1 issues an unparalleled, overt blessing upon anyone who reads and keeps the words of the book of Revelation (Rev 1:3).

Second, studying prophecy heightens our awareness that the world is temporary and deepens our appreciation of the time that we have on Earth. Once we recognize the transitory nature of everything around us, we are better prepared and more hopeful in the face of the abrupt, even violent changes foretold in Scripture. The next few seconds of our lives right now are definitive. For non-Christians, these are precious moments in which to find and form a relationship with Jesus and to be saved from eternal condemnation. For Christians, the treasure of time, however big or small, is a means of investing in our relationship with Jesus and with others.

Third, the study of prophecy is transformative for us personally. When we meditate on the Lord's mind and his will, we are more malleable and willing to let him shape our hearts and minds.[4] Prophecy changes those who read it and apply their minds to understanding it.

---

4. This is further discussed by Pember, *Earth's Earliest Ages*, 12–16.

In all of these benefits, we are growing closer to the Lord and becoming more cognizant of the importance of eternity. The Bible thrusts before us a panoramic "sneak peek" of coming events. As the present fades in comparison to the future, our perspective broadens at the same time as it hones in on Christ. Evangelism becomes more urgent and meaningful. The supernatural becomes more real and active. Prayer becomes more significant and passionate. Studying prophecy is an act of obedience and a privilege that helps us thrive as Christians. It gives God glory and us insight. Romans 16 declares,

> Now to him that is of power to stablish you according to my gospel, and the preaching of Jesus Christ, according to the revelation of the mystery, which was kept secret since the world began, But now is made manifest, and by the scriptures of the prophets, according to the commandment of the everlasting God, made known to all nations for the obedience of faith. (vv. 25–26)

It's to our personal advantage to respond to the Lord's call by opening our eyes and poring over the Scriptures graciously given to us by God. The Bible is a love letter written to anyone who will take heed and read it for what it is. Shouldn't we obey the Lord and put his Word to good use? Hard as it can be to make Bible reading and study a habit, the benefits are beyond compare.

Our forebears in the Church constantly devoted themselves to obedient study of the Bible. When we examine the practices of the apostles and early church, prophetic study reveals itself right at the top of their priorities list. The Gospels are packed with direct quotations from the Old Testament. Well-versed (pun intended) in the Scriptures as they possessed them through the first century, the apostles knew what to expect in and from the Messiah. They did not understand everything, but they had a broad idea of what Jesus Christ would be. In many aspects, they had an exceptionally detailed picture of what the Messiah would be.

The Church's birthday at Pentecost immediately evoked and invoked prophecy. Jesus had ascended into heaven ten days earlier, and now the disciples were gathered in prayer and celebration of the Feast of Pentecost. They were waiting in the city of Jerusalem, as Christ had instructed them to do (Acts 1:4). Meanwhile, Jerusalem was packed with other Jews who had assembled in Jerusalem for Pentecost. The Mosaic law commanded Jewish males to observe Pentecost at the temple (Exod 34:22–23). An agricultural festival, Pentecost was the perfect time for an initial harvest of souls. It was on this day that the Holy Spirit descended upon believers and caused them to speak in tongues. The disciples' sudden ability to speak multiple languages was a gift granted by God and suited for the immediate needs of evangelism on that day.

As the bewildered crowds struggled to make sense of the disciples' newfound capabilities, Peter rose to address the people. He went straight to the Old Testament. "But this is that which was spoken by the prophet Joel," he begins, citing a passage from Joel 2 (Acts 2:16). Peter then describes Jesus' ministry, death, and resurrection before again quoting the Old Testament for context: "For David speaketh concerning him" (Acts 2:25a).

Peter quotes prophecy because he knows it comes directly from the Lord. Explaining David's words from Ps 16, Peter says that David "received of the Father the promise of the Holy Ghost" (Acts 2:33b). Like David, Peter realized that the psalm was divinely inspired. It was a prophecy from God's own mouth.

As time passed, the early Christians continued to put prophecy front and center in their relationship with each other and with the world. Paul is an excellent example of someone who understood the pivotal role that prophecy plays in Christianity. Immediately after his conversion, Paul turns to prophecy to provide evidence for Jesus as the Christ. In Damascus, he "confounded the Jews which dwelt at Damascus, proving that this is very Christ" (Acts 9:22b). In Thessalonica, Paul enters the synagogue and spends three Sabbath days explaining prophecy. He "reasoned with them out of the scriptures," Acts 17 records, "opening and alleging, that Christ must needs have suffered, and risen again from the dead; and that this Jesus, whom I preach unto you, is Christ" (vv. 2b–3). Here, Paul is reasoning with Thessalonians, the same people he writes to in 1 Thess 4. Their willingness to be reading and listening to Scripture is connected to an eagerness for Christ's return.

The truth of prophecy drives Paul forward in urgently sharing the gospel message. Defending himself before King Agrippa, Paul takes the opportunity to speak of salvation through Christ alone. Paul cites prophecy, tying Scripture together with current events so well that he frightens the governor, Festus. Festus accuses Paul of madness. "I am not mad, most noble Festus," Paul calmly replies, "but speak forth the words of truth and soberness" (Acts 26:25b). He then addresses Agrippa: "King Agrippa, believest thou the prophets? I know that thou believest" (Acts 26:27). Agrippa's fascinating answer after such a short time of listening highlights the persuasive power of the evidence Paul presented. Agrippa balks at converting on the spot, but proclaims, "Almost thou persuadest me to be a Christian" (Acts 26:28b). Moreover, once imprisoned in Rome, Paul spends most of his time showing the Jewish leaders how Jesus fulfills prophecy. Each day "he expounded and testified the kingdom of God, persuading them concerning Jesus, both out of the law of Moses, and out of the prophets, from morning till evening" (Acts 28:23b).

These few examples demonstrate how Bible prophecy frames Peter's speech, the birthday of the Church, and the spread of Christianity throughout the Roman Empire, always conveying and heightening the expectation that prophecy is bound to future meaning and anticipation for what is coming. All of this is prophecy cited in fulfillment of the past and with a sense of urgency for the future. The disciples realized that prophecy was being fulfilled before their eyes. Because it was being fulfilled then, it would continue to be fulfilled further. Prophecy known and remembered, prophecy studied and internalized, was necessary for understanding the past, contextualizing the present, and preparing for the future.

In every regard, the Church began with the study and proclamation of prophecy. Prophetic study remained a bedrock of the early church and Christian doctrine. Without prophecy recalled and understood through a biblical lens, no one could have held any expectations about the Messiah, and the Messiah was the only reason that the Church existed.

The apostles repeatedly admonished fellow Christians to pore over the Word of God and the prophecies it contains. James urges believers to meditate on and internalize Scripture:

> Receive with meekness the engrafted word, which is able to save your souls. But be ye doers of the word, and not hearers only, deceiving your own selves. (Jas 1:21b–22)

Similarly, in Colossians, Paul reminds other Christians of the "hope which is laid up for you in heaven, whereof ye heard before in the word of the truth of the gospel" (1:5b). Time after time, the early church was instructed to pay attention to what the Lord had said in his written Word and through Jesus Christ, the Word incarnate. Nothing was supposed to be done without constant, prayerful, and intentional focus on the prophecies given by God to his people in Scripture. Hebrews 4 emphasizes the power of the Bible: "For the word of God is quick, and powerful, and sharper than any twoedged sword, piercing even to the dividing asunder of soul and spirit, and of the joints and marrow, and is a discerner of the thoughts and intents of the heart" (Heb 4:12).

Reflection Questions:

1. How and where does the book of Acts convey the disciples' excitement about Jesus' return?

2. Consider Isa 9:6–7, a passage routinely read during Christmas celebrations. What parts of these verses were fulfilled in the First Coming? What parts are left to be fulfilled?

3. Review Peter's speech in Acts 2. How many allusions do you find to passages and promises from the Old Testament?

4. Read Eph 5:21–33. The Bible describes the Church as Jesus' Bride. Based on this passage from Eph, what sort of relationship do a husband and wife have in a healthy marriage? How can Christians foster a similar relationship with Jesus the Groom?

5. In 1 Thessalonians, Paul is assuring other Christians that God has not forgotten deceased believers. Believers who pass away before the Rapture occurs are instantly with Jesus in heaven (as also expressed in Phil 1:23 and 2 Cor 5:8, for example), even though their physical remains are still waiting for the glorious moment of transformation at his coming (as seen in verses such as 1 Cor 15:51–53 and 1 Thess 4:16–17). How does 2 Cor 4–5 reinforce our expectation that we will be made new?

6. In the Gospels, Jesus regularly quotes from the Old Testament or speaks of fulfilling prophecy. Many Bibles have footnotes with references for the passages he cites. Take time today to find one of those footnotes and follow it back to the Old Testament, reading the original verse in its earlier context. Next, read the entire Old Testament chapter containing that verse. How does Jesus fulfill the verse or the prophecy associated with it?

13

Imminency and the Christian's Action Plan

> Behold, I come quickly: hold that fast which thou hast, that no man take thy crown. (Rev 3:11)

FOLLOWING IN THE FOOTSTEPS of the early church, let's consider the three components of the Philadelphian promise as they opened the last chapter. There, we called the Rapture promise a reminder of three things: (*a*) we should endeavor to be faithful through trials; (*b*) we have a greater promise that should encourage us; and (*c*) we need to be evangelizing and sharing the gospel. These three aspects of anticipation spurred the early church on in their love for Christ and for others. Everything in Philadelphian Christianity—everything in Christianity—is, after all, about Jesus. Keeping Jesus at the center of our focus, this three-part reminder continues to offer us an action plan for Philadelphian Christianity, with an imminency mindset that is as valid today as it has ever been.

First, realizing that Jesus is coming at any moment, Philadelphian Christianity is faithful in the tribulations that occur before he comes. Nothing prevents Jesus from returning at any moment for the Church. Passages such as Matt 24 describe the Rapture as an event that will occur when it is least expected, but when the world has fallen into complete spiritual disarray. It will be a time like the days of Noah. People will be actively engaged in life, living in sin, and not realizing that judgment is impending (vv. 37–41). "Watch therefore: for ye know not what hour your Lord doth come," Jesus tells the disciples (v. 42). In Matt 25, shortly afterward, he repeats the instruction. "Watch therefore, for ye know neither the day nor the hour wherein the Son of man cometh" (v. 13). His people should be ready, because he will come for the Church at any second.

Further, until Jesus does come, we know to expect trials and tribulations. In 1 Peter, Peter reminds Christians that trials will result in a treasure more precious than any earthly gold. The treasure, he explains, is full of "praise and honour and glory at the appearing of Jesus Christ" (1:7b). In troubles, our concentration should be on what we know about God and his character. Whatever else, the Lord is good, has the best in store, and uses tribulations for our advantage. Romans 8:28b assures believers that "all things work together for good to them that love God, to them who are the called according to his purpose." That purpose, although it may not feel good and comforting in the moment, results in God's further glory and our closer alignment to Christ. Through hardships and the other experiences the Lord allows in our lives, we are continuously being "conformed to the image of his Son" (Rom 8:29b). Likewise, Jesus tells the disciples that the Lord prunes and purges fruitful believers so that they may bear more fruit (John 15:2). As Paul and Barnabas reminded other believers, "we must through much tribulation enter into the kingdom of God" (Acts 14:22b). Far from being immune from troubles, the Church is warned to expect a whole host of tribulations while waiting for Jesus.

Endurance is a very hard teaching. It's much easier to say than to do. Certainly, we will fall short and feel that we fail in it. Nonetheless, it can help to remember that we are not alone in the struggles we face. The Lord is faithful to be with us and not remove his promises. His promises are fulfilled *through* tribulations, not *in spite of* tribulations (John 16:33, 1 Cor 10:13, 2 Cor 12:9). In the worst of circumstances, "we are more than conquerors through him that loved us" (Rom 8:37b). God sees our sufferings. Nothing comes to or against us without his knowledge.

Moreover, according to 1 Peter, the Lord is going through our trials with us, and has a specific purpose in mind. "But the God of all grace, who hath called us unto his eternal glory by Christ Jesus, after that ye have suffered a while, make you perfect, stablish, strengthen, settle you" (5:10). Earlier in the same chapter, 1 Peter expresses how vital it is to commit ourselves to God in all things:

IMMINENCY AND THE CHRISTIAN'S ACTION PLAN

> Humble yourselves therefore under the mighty hand of God, that he may exalt you in due time: Casting all your care upon him; for he careth for you. (5:6–7)

Christianity is entirely reliant on Jesus Christ for salvation in the first place. Philadelphian Christianity—that is, healthy Christianity for daily living and missions—abides in Christ by abiding in this absolute dependency on Jesus. In our trials and tribulations, Ps 34 reminds us that "the Lord redeemeth the soul of his servants: and none of them that trust in him shall be desolate" (v. 22). Tribulations do not have to tear us away from God. They ought to drive us toward him. According to Prov 18:10, "The name of the Lord is a strong tower: the righteous runneth into it, and is safe." Jesus is the Lord, and we know him by name. He is Yeshua, whose name literally means "salvation." Our strong tower is salvation through Jesus Christ alone. When we take shelter in the salvation he brings and find our righteousness in him, we are safe. We are sheltering under his name and the power of his blood.

Not only are we not alone because the Lord is with us, but we also have other kinds of community to be found in our hardships. First Peter reminds us that in our tribulations we have fellowship together as Christians.

> Be sober, be vigilant; because your adversary the devil, as a roaring lion, walketh about, seeking whom he may devour: Whom resist stedfast in the faith, knowing that the same afflictions are accomplished in your brethren that are in the world. (5:8–9)

Our fellow Christians worldwide are going through trials and tribulations. It may feel like we are alone in spiritual warfare, but we are not. The entire book of 1 Peter is written to Christians who are about to undergo intense persecution under Emperor Nero. These early believers were all about to suffer a grueling trial together, although they could not yet know its extent and severity.

Perhaps the most helpful truth to remember is why Christians face trials and tribulations at all, either individually or collectively. Why does the devil prowl around believers in particular? Why does the world have such antipathy for Christians? Jesus answers:

> If the world hate you, ye know that it hated me before it hated you. If ye were of the world, the world would love his own: but because ye are not of the world, but I have chosen you out of the world, therefore the world hateth you. Remember the word that

> I said unto you, The servant is not greater than his lord. If they have persecuted me, they will also persecute you; if they have kept my saying, they will keep yours also. But all these things will they do unto you for my name's sake, because they know not him that sent me. (John 15:18–21)

The world and its ruler hate Christians because they hate our King. Recalling that we suffer persecution because of our King and not because of ourselves, and that our King is who he is, Philadelphian Christianity focuses on the King and strives to be faithful in all trials and tribulations. It turns our eyes back to Christ as our Lord and Sovereign.

Reflecting on the King and his character leads back to the second aspect of Philadelphian Christianity. The Church enjoys the unique promise of the Rapture. First Thessalonians 4 is a passage of encouragement. When the Christians in Thessalonica are downhearted, Paul reminds them of the promise of the Rapture. In addition, they do not have to be discouraged or fearful for believers who have died before them, because there is an assurance that extends to all of Jesus' people, regardless of the Rapture. All Christians, whenever they have lived and died, will ultimately be with Christ.

For Christians, this powerful reminder can provide solace and direction for every moment of life and death. Jesus' promise to return is a comfort when facing the sorrow of death and the uncertainties of life. The Rapture is a special assurance that Jesus can come at any time. It is very physical and, someday, will be very tangible. Beyond that, however, whenever we live or die as Christians, we have the promise of eternal life. What a blessing, greater than we could ever hope to achieve or earn!

Second Corinthians 4 ties together this future hope and the encouragement to persevere through trials.

> For our light affliction, which is but for a moment, worketh for us a far more exceeding and eternal weight of glory; While we look not at the things which are seen, but at the things which are not seen: for the things which are seen are temporal; but the things which are not seen are eternal. (vv. 17–18)

The Philadelphian Christian mindset is fixed on the future. Rather than looking only to today, it sees tomorrow, as well. Yet its true future vision is found in seeing through the lens of Jesus Christ. Through that lens, tomorrow is not about tomorrow on this earth, but tomorrow as in millions of years from now. What is eternal outweighs what is temporal.

IMMINENCY AND THE CHRISTIAN'S ACTION PLAN

Reflecting on eternity in this way, Philadelphian Christianity concentrates its efforts and thoughts on what is to come.

Paul comments on this lens for eternity in Phil 3. He notes that it is a habit to cultivate and a discipline to pursue. It requires looking ahead to what we will be in the future, through Christ, instead of what we once were in the past, apart from him. "Brethren, I count not myself to have apprehended," Paul remarks, "but this one thing I do, forgetting those things which are behind, and reaching forth unto those things which are before" (v. 13). Paul's goal is the "prize of the high calling of God in Christ Jesus" (v. 14b). This mindset, he affirms, is a mature mindset.

Following this model of maturity, we are intended to focus on the eternal and unseen by fixing our eyes on the God who stepped into our world and revealed himself to us in Jesus: "For God, who commanded the light to shine out of darkness, hath shined in our hearts, *to give the light of the knowledge of the glory of God in the face of Jesus Christ*" (2 Cor 4:6, italics added).

Our action plan for Philadelphian Christianity cannot be separated from a healthy obsession with the Word of God in written form (the Bible) and human form (Jesus Christ). Since the Bible is the inspired Word of God, and since Jesus is the Word of God in living flesh, Jesus' teachings in Scripture will never contradict any other verses in the Bible. His character is completely consistent with the rest of what we see, hear, and read about God. We are waiting every second to see him in physical form. With that expectation in mind, we should strive to be reading, studying, and enjoying the love letter the Lord wrote to us in the Bible.

Living as if Jesus is coming at any second inspires the third distinctive element of Philadelphian Christianity: missions and evangelism. For the Philadelphian, evangelism starts at home. Living out the teachings of the Word is a necessity and a privilege. Watching how we live in Jesus, others will hopefully recognize there is something different about us, and will be encouraged to look more deeply into learning what drives that difference.

Christians are supposed to let our light shine by allowing the light of Jesus to shine through us. A light is designed to illuminate its surroundings, not to be hidden away. As Jesus puts it,

> Ye are the light of the world. A city that is set on an hill cannot be hid. Neither do men light a candle, and put it under a bushel, but on a candlestick; and it giveth light unto all that are in the house.

> Let your light so shine before men, that they may see your good works, and glorify your Father which is in heaven. (Matt 5:14–16)

As often as we read these verses, we might not notice how they refer both to individual lifestyles and to our fellowship with other Christians. In Rev 1, the apostle John has a vision of the Lord Jesus walking in the midst of seven golden candlesticks (vv. 12–13). Jesus explains that the seven candlesticks are the seven churches (v. 20). Expounding on the seven churches, Rev 2–3 show what kinds of churches exist, how they relate to Jesus, and how they compare to one other. The positive and negative models of these churches also help us to understand our role as light in the world.

At the moment of personal salvation, we automatically come into the Church Invisible. We are part of the Body of Christ, his Bride, the Church. Accordingly, we are a light being set upon a candlestick. The Church is the candlestick revealing Christians to the world.

That is to say that, on a more visible level, the church institutions and types seen in Rev 2–3 are candlesticks that showcase us to the world. When we join or attend a church, our light is being placed on display. A healthy, thriving church will be a proper candlestick for sharing light with the world. As we complement others in a healthy church community, our light shines even brighter and bolder for all to see, drawing their eyes to the truth. By contrast, unhealthy churches—fake churches, groups that gather to practice nominal Christianity or even to blaspheme God in the name of supposed worship—are candlesticks that can be removed by Jesus himself (Rev 2:5).

As individuals and as units, we want to endeavor to be a bright candle on a strong candlestick. As Philadelphian Christians, we should endeavor to seek out fellowship with like-minded Christians who are growing toward Christ, challenging themselves to read and study, and eagerly awaiting his impending return.

> Let us hold fast the profession of our faith without wavering; (for he is faithful that promised;) And let us consider one another to provoke unto love and to good works: Not forsaking the assembling of ourselves together, as the manner of some is; but exhorting one another: and so much the more, as ye see the day approaching. (Heb 10:23–25)

In all of these areas, the Bible emphasizes intentionality. Christians must put our energy into following Jesus Christ. As we get to know Jesus more and more closely, our anticipation for his return builds. The more time and effort we put into aligning ourselves with Scripture, the more we will be watching to see Jesus come, and the more excited we will be about spending eternity with him.

The intentional lifestyle of Philadelphian Christianity is comprehensive. It relates to the heart, mind, soul, and strength. In short, it shows that we need to be examining our own hearts, paying attention to what sort of fellowship we are choosing, and concentrating first and foremost on Jesus as the coming Lord and Savior—because we cannot wait to see him face to face.

Reflection Questions:

1. What does it mean to talk about the "imminency" of Jesus' return? Consider John 14 and Jesus' words to the disciples.

2. As a promise of physical deliverance and removal from Earth, the Rapture is a unique kind of promise. Why would the apostles and early church have been especially excited about the Rapture?

3. When you think about the future, how far ahead do you automatically visualize? A few days, a few years, a few decades? How far ahead does the Bible encourage us to think?

4. Read Matt 5–7. How does the Sermon on the Mount emphasize a practical Philadelphian Christian mindset?

5. As an experiment, set a recurring reminder on your phone: "Jesus is coming any minute." Try using the reminder every day at noon for a week. How did having a daily prompt affect you? Did it change your outlook or make you think more urgently about the need to share the gospel? Why or why not?

6. Read 2 Pet 3:13–14 aloud. If you knew that Jesus was coming back in exactly two hours, would it affect your idea of prayer? What sort of heart would you want to have at the moment of his return?

14

Citizens of God's Country

> *Him that overcometh will I make a pillar in the temple of my God,* and he shall go no more out: and I will write upon him the name of my God, and the name of the city of my God, which is new Jerusalem, which cometh down out of heaven from my God: and I will write upon him my new name. —Rev 3:12[1]

EACH OF THE CHURCH letters in Rev 2–3 contains a promise for those who overcome the world and are faithful to Jesus the Messiah. Jesus only expects that we as his people do our best to follow him, despite our repeat failures and inherent imperfection. The Philadelphian overcomers' promise emphasizes permanency, privilege, and belonging. Jesus' encouragement meets the thriving church where it is spiritually, corresponding perfectly to their relationship with him. Speaking of the overcomer, Christ says, "him that overcometh will I make a pillar in the temple of my God, and he shall go no more out: and I will write upon him the name of my God, and the name of the city of my God, which is new Jerusalem, which cometh down out of heaven from my God: and I will write upon him my new name" (Rev 3:12).

The Philadelphian Christian will be made a pillar in God's temple and will never again leave his presence. For people living in a territory that had suffered intense structural damage from earthquakes, the promise of becoming an unshakeable pillar would doubtlessly be uplifting! The

---

1. Italics added.

Philadelphians find in Christ a steadiness and permanency that transcend any threat. After its tremendous early first-century earthquake, residents of Philadelphia seem to have been particularly affected by the fear of tremors and structural instability. Many Philadelphians stayed outside the city to be safer. Jesus' assurance of going out no more contrasts with their immediate situation. Secure in his presence, no Philadelphian Christian will ever have to seek any other shelter. "The victor shall be shaken by no disaster in the great day of trial; and he shall never again require to go out and take refuge in the open country."[2]

Jesus' words offer the promise of remaining with the Lord and maintaining an intimate relationship with him. Physically, it is a promise of remaining with the Lord and literally staying with him forever. It recalls David's longing to be with God: "One thing have I desired of the Lord, that will I seek after; that I may dwell in the house of the Lord all the days of my life, to behold the beauty of the Lord, and to enquire in his temple" (Ps 27:4). For the Lord's people, it is a joy to be with him. Eternity in his intimate presence is the greatest reward.

With the reference to the pillar, Jesus' pledge to the overcomer has a physical foreshadowing in the Old Testament. The promise hearkens back to the description of the First Temple in Jerusalem. First Kings 5–8 and 2 Chr 2–8 give the account of the First Temple's construction, which took place in the tenth century BC under the direction of King Solomon. Two special bronze pillars stand in the lavish temple's courtyard. Each pillar is twenty-seven feet high and is topped by a decorative capital featuring lilies and pomegranates (1 Kgs 7:15–22). The pillars were destroyed by the Chaldeans when they razed the First Temple in the sixth century. (By that time, the pillars were hollow. This is probably because most of the bronze had been repurposed, likely by relatively impoverished apostate kings seeking out precious materials; see Jer 52:20–23.)

Standing immovably in the courtyard, the pillars are an embellishment. Inasmuch as they do not hold up any part of the temple structure, they serve no architectural purpose. But do they have a prophetic purpose? Since every detail of Scripture and of the First Temple is important, this is a good question to ask ourselves of any puzzle in the Bible. The allusion in Rev 3 indicates that there may be more to the physical pillars than we might at first think.

---

2. Ramsay, *Letters to the Seven Churches*, 408.

The pillars do turn out to have a distinctive purpose, even if it is not as obvious as supporting the temple's roof. Enticing the eye, they add to the glory of the temple. They enhance the courtyard by imposing a sense of awe upon visitors. Of course, the pillars are not part of the First Temple's necessary design. The temple can stand without them. In that sense, being self-sufficient, the temple does not need them. The pillars, on the other hand, do need the temple. No one is traveling to Jerusalem solely to visit the spectacular bronze pillars.

As an adornment chosen by the architect, as a symbolic element of beauty, the pillars illustrate the wealth and foresight involved in the First Temple. They fully belong to the temple; they would have no reason for existing, apart from it. Again, no ancients journeyed to Jerusalem just in order to view Solomon's fine pillars. The physical pillars hint at the further glory inside the temple.

The relationship between the pillars and the temple corresponds to our relationship with the Lord. Sinners are saved when they come to admire and worship Christ, not when they worship Christ's people. No one becomes a Christian in order to admire other Christians. Like the pillars, we are adornments that highlight God's greatness, not our own. The glory of the Father is revealed in us as believers. Although God is complete in himself because he is holy, he shares his glory through the redemption and rich inheritance we receive in him. As living pillars, we both exhibit and enjoy God's beauty.

Since God is complete and self-sufficient, he does not need us to "hold him up" any more than the physical temple architecturally requires the courtyard pillars. God as architect creates us to be embellishments of his courtyard and never to leave his presence. We are shaped by his design, but not by his need. As the pillars belong wholly to the temple and serve a single purpose related to its glory, so too do we belong completely to the Lord and exist in order to display and promote his glory. He takes pleasure in us.

The pillars' names are equally deliberate and meaningful. The two names communicate the message of the gospel, which reveals God's glory through and in his people. One pillar is called Jachin; the other, Boaz (1 Kgs 7:21). Jachin means "he shall establish." Jachin alludes to steadfastness. Boaz means "strength" or "in it is strength" and refers to strength and quickness.[3]

---

[3]. Cf. Orr, s.v. "Jachin and Boaz."

Who establishes these aptly-named pillars? Who has imbued them with any strength? Because they are standing in the amazing temple courtyard in the blessed city of Jerusalem, the biblical answer is that the *Lord* establishes them. The pillars proclaim that God provides and sustains. He gifts us with both physical and spiritual strength.

The physical pillars' purpose runs parallel to the Church's purpose. Both the pillars and the Church exist to declare God's majesty. Matthew 16 describes God's provision in reference to the establishment of Christ's Body. According to Matt 16:16–18, the Church is built on Christ, the Rock. In this passage, Peter professes Jesus as the Christ, the Son of God. Jesus responds by reminding Peter that Peter's own name is a pun on the rock (John 1:42). In the Greek, Peter's name magnifies Christ as the One who establishes. Whereas the name Peter is the Greek word πέτρος, or *petros*, referring to a small stone, the Rock on which the Church is built is πέτρα, *petra*. The *petra* is a fixed stone or a ledge. It is a firm rock in a set place. As the Rock, Jesus is a firm foundation (Matt 7:24–25). Jesus was revealing himself as the Messiah who would establish and strengthen all who come to him in faith. The household of God boasts Jesus as its "chief corner stone" (Eph 2:20b).

Matthew 16 goes on to show the authority and strength of Jesus Christ the Rock, indisputable Son of the Living God (Matt 16:16). In v. 19, Jesus speaks of the strength and authority that he imparts to his people: "And I will give unto thee the keys of the kingdom of heaven: and whatsoever thou shalt bind on earth shall be bound in heaven: and whatsoever thou shalt loose on earth shall be loosed in heaven." Rev 3:7 has already evoked a similar promise spoken to the Philadelphians. Jesus has the key of David and controls all access. What Jesus establishes cannot be undone; what he opens and shuts cannot be forced the other way (Rev 3:7–8). He holds all authority, as he tells the disciples before he ascends to heaven: "All power is given unto me in heaven and in earth" (Matt 28:18b).

The pillars in Solomon's Temple do not actively support the temple, and we as the Body of Christ do not support Jesus. The physical pillars in the temple courtyard are symbolic. Their entire purpose is to become part of the visible fellowship and glory of God. Again, the Bible stresses that this is like our purpose as believers. The Church displays the "manifest wisdom of God" (Eph 3:10b). The Lord creates his people for his glory (Isa 43:6–7).

Keeping God's Word and observing his commands to share the gospel and love one another, the Philadelphians demonstrate his strength in their weakness. They are firmly established in Christ, who has full authority. Like the pillars, they remain in the Lord's presence. They have ongoing fellowship with God and enjoy the access and opportunity he has granted them. Notably, even for us today, the Philadelphians persist as pillars of the faith. They display the glory of God in Rev 3!

The pillar promise to the Philadelphians captures a glimpse of their eternal outcome. Christians have the assurance of living in eternity with Christ. Eternity is described for us in Rev 21–22, where John talks about the future city of the new Jerusalem. The new Jerusalem is a beautiful, pure city of perfect proportions. Built of precious gems and pearly gates, it contains no temple structure. John comments, "And I saw no temple therein: for the Lord God Almighty and the Lamb are the temple of it" (Rev 21:22).

Philadelphian Christians have the guarantee that the Lord God and the Lamb are the temple of the future city, where all Christians will dwell forever. The Philadelphians are told that they will abide in the Lord, who is the temple. They will never be cast out of his presence, but will forever display his glory and beauty. He establishes them in strength, just as the pillars Jachin and Boaz demonstrate in a literal sense with the physical temple.

Other qualities of the pillars foreshadow the Philadelphian mindset and Jesus' letter to the church. Cast of molten bronze, Jachin and Boaz are formed of a material that has been through the fire. Christians with a little strength who have kept Christ's word have been through a spiritual fire of temptation, testing, and purification. In their endurance, they are cast of molten bronze. Their patience has a purpose that glorifies God: they bear fruit because they have been pruned by the Lord as he uses them for service and his honor (John 15:2).

As the pillars are intended to stand, Christians who keep Jesus' commands are bearing fruit that will last. This fruit is the good work that we are created to do for Jesus by loving him, treasuring him as Lord and Savior, and consequently doing as he would have us do, now that we seek to please him. We believe that he is worth obeying (Heb 11:6, Eph 2:8–10). First Corinthians characterizes such good works as those that will last because they are done for Christ as on the foundation of Christ:

> For other foundation can no man lay than that is laid, which is Jesus Christ. Now if any man build upon this foundation gold, silver, precious stones, wood, hay, stubble; Every man's work shall be made manifest: for the day shall declare it, because it shall be revealed by fire; and the fire shall try every man's work of what sort it is. If any man's work abide which he hath built thereupon, he

> shall receive a reward. If any man's work shall be burned, he shall suffer loss: but he himself shall be saved; yet so as by fire. (3:11–15)

Bronze is tried by fire and shows its strength. Made of bronze, Jachin and Boaz have been through fire and show strength in the temple courtyard. Christians are likewise refined by allowing themselves to be weak in Christ's strength. Persevering in affliction bears fruit and builds a firmer relationship with God. The Philadelphian Christians reflect these qualities in their character, as manifest in their lives. And as the pillars are further embellished with their own exceptional, decorative features, we as Christians should be adorned as the Lord would have us be, with beauty that reveals his beauty.

The adornment of the pillars in the First Temple's courtyard looks ahead to the specific qualities that the Lord instills in Philadelphian Christians. The pillars are decorated with embossed lilies and pomegranates. In Solomon's time, lilies were associated with luxuriousness and life. Lilies thrived in thorny valleys and were a clean white or a fresh scarlet color, testifying to the cleanliness of hearts washed pure in Jesus' blood. Pomegranates, in turn, are a fruit associated with richness and wealth.[4] Their deep colors and flavor signify luxury and abundance.

The biblical book Song of Solomon features both lilies and pomegranates in its imagery of lushness and luxury. Lilies and pomegranates appear in many verses, such as Song 2:1–2; 5:13; 6:2 (lilies); and Song 4:13, 6:11, and 7:12 (pomegranates). Song of Solomon is a short book focusing on the depths of love. Prophetically, this Old Testament book speaks of the bountiful, regal love that Christ has for his people. In light of the Song of Solomon, it's no surprise that lilies and pomegranates are decorative features of the pillars in Solomon's Temple! God extends extravagant love to us by reaching out through Christ. As pillars in God's courtyard, the Philadelphian Christians will be decorated with his loving richness and the abundant wealth of God's glory.

The overcomer of Philadelphia, compared to an immovable pillar, has a marvelous decoration. "I will write upon him the name of my God," the Lord states, "and the name of the city of my God, which is new Jerusalem, which cometh down out of heaven from my God: and I will write upon him my new name" (Rev 3:12b). While Jesus does not mention lilies and pomegranates, the imagery of love, abundance, and pleasure is evocative of Song of Solomon. Exhibiting love and bounty, the primary

---

4. Cf. Orr, s.vv. "Pomegranate," "Lily"; Got Questions, "Significance of Pomegranates."

decoration of the pillar in the new Jerusalem is just as precious in God's sight. Rather than earthly symbols or objects, the Philadelphian inscriptions will be a series of names. Yet these are not any ordinary names. They are marks of eternity, belonging, and permanency.

The Philadelphian Christian who abides in God's presence will bear three glorious inscriptions. The first is the name of God. Being labeled first and prominently with God's name signifies that the Lord establishes the Philadelphian Christian. In ancient architecture, and not uncommonly today, a public structure has columns, bricks, or another element permanently emblazoned with the name of someone associated with that structure. The name may be inscribed as a mark of honor for a person who has donated money, designed the building, or happened to hold an important office at the time.

One example of such an inscription is found on the portico of the pagan temple called the Pantheon, in Rome. A columned porch area attached to the front of the Pantheon, the portico is older than the rest of the surviving building. Marcus Agrippa (ca. 63–12 BC), a chief official and close friend of the first Roman emperor Augustus, had commissioned an earlier temple that originally stood on the site. The first Pantheon bore Agrippa's name on the front of the building. Written in large letters, the abbreviated Latin inscription reads, *M.AGRIPPA.L.F.COS.TERTIUM.FECIT*. The compact sentence translates to "Marcus Agrippa, Lucius's son, made this when he was consul for the third time." Even though the Pantheon standing today dates to about one hundred fifty years after the portico, the portico was deliberately left with its original inscription. The signed portico was intended to be a perpetual honor for Agrippa as the first builder of the Pantheon.

An inscription is a brand of honor and ownership. The inscription that names a project's architect or other powerful advocate conveys even more acclaim than the building does, and communicates the glory of the builder over the building. As the book of Hebrews reminds us, "he who hath builded the house hath more honour than the house" (Heb 3:3b). Through an inscription, the building becomes a greater symbol of the builder's importance, power, and resources. The inscription on God's buildings, his people, has a similar effect and function. Who is the builder of the Christian? God himself, of course (Heb 3:4; 1 Cor 3:9, 16). The Lord receives the glory for and in us, the work of his hands. The Philadelphian overcomer can rejoice in knowing that God's own name is going to be written on him in the new Jerusalem.

Revelation 22 shows the fulfillment of the promise made to the Philadelphians. Once the curse of sin and decay has passed away, there will be an eternal new heaven and earth.

> And there shall be no more curse: but the throne of God and of the Lamb shall be in it; and his servants shall serve him: And they shall see his face; and his name shall be in their foreheads. (vv. 3–4)

God's name is inscribed on his people's foreheads. If that fact seems insignificant, consider what an honor it is. Imagine that God should be willing to demonstrate that he has designed us as his own people and that he claims us as his own! Not only has he made us, but he is also not ashamed to publicize that we belong to him. He is actually proud to call us his.

A mark of citizenship and a close connection to the King, the honor of the inscription demonstrates how much the Christian's allegiance matters to God. Since believers simply want to be with God, they seek after his city and his country. Hebrews 11 states, "But now they desire a better country, that is, an heavenly: wherefore God is not ashamed to be called their God: for he hath prepared for them a city" (v. 16). The inscription is an honorific, a stamp of ownership, and a declaration of satisfaction with one's work. What a beautiful and merciful promise, coming straight from the lips of the Lord God Almighty.

In Rev 3, Jesus promises that the second inscription on the Philadelphian overcomer is "the name of the city of my God." According to Rev 21–22, God's city is the new Jerusalem. The new Jerusalem is the eternal home of Jesus' Bride and of all those who across the ages have believed in Jesus Christ as Lord and Savior. Through faith in God's messianic promises, Old Testament saints found salvation in Jesus; through faith in the Messiah who has come by name, died, and risen again, the New Testament saints still today find salvation in Jesus. Through faith in the Messiah, others after the Rapture will come to be saved; these believers are the Tribulation saints. For all of the saints, salvation is the promise of perfect eternal life with the Lord.

Purity and holiness are hallmarks of the new Jerusalem. A magnificent city untouched by sin and untainted by death, the new Jerusalem is where "the tabernacle of God is with men, and he will dwell with them, and they shall be his people, and God himself shall be with them, and be their God" (Rev 21:3b). We cannot fathom what we will witness in the new Jerusalem and eternity, but we can expect it to include riches of grace and glory forever. Ephesians says,

> But God, who is rich in mercy, for his great love wherewith he loved us, Even when we were dead in sins, hath quickened us together with Christ, (by grace ye are saved;) And hath raised us up together, and made us sit together in heavenly places in Christ Jesus: That in the ages to come he might shew the exceeding riches of his grace in his kindness toward us through Christ Jesus. (2:4–7)

Citizenship bestows exclusive belonging and benefits. As a citizen of the new Jerusalem, the Philadelphian overcomer enjoys the promise of bearing the eternal city's name. He has all the privileges of living in the new Jerusalem. He is under the Lord's protection and will always dwell in perfect peace and joy. Revelation 21 foretells, "And God shall wipe away all tears from their eyes; and there shall be no more death, neither sorrow, nor crying, neither shall there be any more pain: for the former things are passed away" (v. 4). Revelation 22 places a special blessing on the citizens of the city. "Blessed are they that do his commandments, that they may have right to the tree of life, and may enter in through the gates into the city" (v. 14).

The third inscription mentioned in the Rev 3:12 promise is Jesus' new name. We can say very little about this name, except that it must be inexorably bound to the wonders of an amazingly glorious, everlasting display of God's character. Jesus' name will reflect his eternal power and faithfulness. Therefore, it must involve a greater joy and delight than we can imagine, far less describe. "But as it is written, Eye hath not seen, nor ear heard, neither have entered into the heart of man, the things which God hath prepared for them that love him" (1 Cor 2:9, citing Isa 64:4).

For the Philadelphians, bearing Jesus' new name elicits another immediate contrast. After the great Lydian earthquake of AD 17, Roman Emperor Tiberius assisted Philadelphia and the other cities in their recovery. He was so generous that the cities sponsored a Roman monument in his honor. Additionally, Philadelphia founded a cult after Tiberius's adopted son Germanicus, then went so far as to rename the city after the royal family. Philadelphia adopted a new name in recognition of Tiberius, the Caesar, or "king." Philadelphia called itself "Neocaesarea," meaning "New Caesar." Coins from the time indicate that the new name lasted until about AD 42–50.[5] Later, under Emperor Vespasian (AD 70–79), founder of the Flavian family dynasty, the city of Philadelphia temporarily assumed the name "Flavia." The title "Flavia" is found on coins as late as the third century

---

5. Philadelphia's new names and coinage are explored by Ramsay, *Letters to the Seven Churches*, 397–98, 409–11.

AD. William Ramsay remarks upon the significance of Philadelphia's new names, pointing out that the monikers were intended to ally the city strongly with the imperial rulers, their supposed gods.[6]

The Philadelphians living in the city might well see the irony in Jesus' words! Even as their city attempted to rebrand itself after the allegedly divine royal family, the Christians of the city received a promise that they would bear the name of God. Secular Philadelphia tried to connect with kings and fake gods. Philadelphian Christians had the real connection with the King of kings and the one true God. Secular Philadelphia's new names faded away; Philadelphian Christians' new names would and will last.

The name of Jesus is mysterious and wonderful. Remarkably, Rev 19 refers to a name written upon Jesus as he comes riding in judgment at the end of our age: "He had a name written, that no man knew, but he himself" (Rev 19:12b). It's all too easy to presume that we know everything about Jesus, but the fact is that we as fallen humans cannot begin to understand him. We'll have all of eternity to enjoy him for who he is. God is a Mover, Shaker, Creator, Builder, Architect, Designer, Artist. Jesus and his new name are beyond us and our wildest dreams, to be sure, but will endure forever!

Sadly, we shortchange God and eternity by putting God in a box and thinking too little of both him and heaven. In part, we honestly cannot help it. Constrained by images of heavenly harps and puffy clouds, and bound by our perceptions of time and space, we cannot escape our human limitations. But in our weakness we can seek to find pleasure in the promises of the Lord. Heaven is more than mere harps and clouds, and eternity is more than earthly time and space. Heaven, the believer's eternal dwelling, is a place of incomparable excitement and glories. Jesus' new name is a promise that peeks over today's landscape and into tomorrow's horizon. We cannot see past our own world and our own understanding to grasp it. Thankfully, the Philadelphian church could rest on Jesus' promise, knowing that the Lord is unchanging. So can we, too, find rest, knowing that the promise of Jesus' new name represents an everlasting home for us.

The overcomer's promise for Philadelphian Christianity is expansive. Every time we fancy that we know all there is to know about it, there is more. There is citizenship, identity, belonging, mercy, joy, peace. There is God, heaven, the fellowship of eternity with Jesus Christ. There is the removal of the curse and of the shame of sin. There is the delight of having all in all as we remain in the Lord's presence and good pleasure. This is

---

6. Ramsay, *Letters to the Seven Churches*, 397–98, 409–11.

a truly incomprehensible promise of all things new and all things good. Remembering that a trademark of Philadelphian Christianity is the expectation that Jesus could return any minute, we can take this promise as almost palpable. The next phase might begin at any moment. "Surely I come quickly," Jesus vows (Rev 22:20b). The Philadelphian Christian cannot wait, and yet is waiting every single second, crying out, "Amen. Even so, come, Lord Jesus!" (Rev 22:20c).

Reflection Questions:

1. What kind of challenges does a Philadelphian overcomer face?
2. The pillars in the First Temple did not support the temple structure. How is this historical detail important for the Revelation overcomer's comparison to a pillar?
3. How did the pillars in the First Temple's courtyard reflect the glory of the temple?
4. Read Eph 4. How do Christians reflect the glory of God when we are focused on him?
5. In John 10, Jesus declares that he is the Good Shepherd. His followers are the sheep of his flock. What are some ways in which a shepherd asserts ownership over his sheep? What sort of relationship do the sheep and shepherd have in John 10?
6. There is no higher name than the name of Jesus Christ. As a Christian, you have Christ in your name and already inscribed on your heart. As an exercise, select three Bible verses about belonging to God. Read one with each meal or with another activity that you perform at least once in the morning, afternoon, and evening. How does God's ownership of you impact your life all day? Does it convict or comfort you to remember the truth that you belong to him?

Epilogue

Continuing on the Philadelphian-Wannabe Journey

> He that hath an ear, let him hear what the Spirit saith unto the churches. —Rev 3:13

HAVING READ THROUGH THE entire letter to the Philadelphian church, we now come to the capstone, a concluding phrase echoed at the end of every letter to every church in Rev 2–3: "He that hath an ear, let him hear what the Spirit saith unto the churches" (Rev 3:13). Even a short survey of the seven churches reveals how each letter is indeed written to a local, historical church in Asia Minor. The churches refer to the physical, first-century, real-life churches of Ephesus, Smyrna, Pergamon, Thyatira, Sardis, Philadelphia, and Laodicea. In addition, as we've observed, each letter is more broadly intended for the Church as the Body of Christ. For us in our individual fellowships in the church institution, these letters help gauge the health of the local church, denominations, and study groups. What do we need to see changed in ourselves? What matters to Christ? What practical steps can we take to submit ourselves to the Lord and let him do a new work in us together, as a whole? The letters raise these questions and more.

Further, we see that the seven letters reflect the development of the church institution across history. Following the letters from start to finish, the institution of the Church Visible is marching increasingly onward into the days of the last-days church of Laodicea. This final church is a church of nominal Christianity. Marked by emptiness and smug self-deception, the Laodicean church is blinded by its desire to please itself and to form friendships with the world. Its alliances are made out of fleshly lusts, rather than from turning to the Lord and Savior who requires a separation from our sinful nature. Jesus wants us to choose to follow him and to live out that choice. Laodicea refuses. Adhering to its own ideas of right and wrong, Laodicea lives in sin and affirms evil. The Laodicean church institution claims to be loving and godly but prizes sin over souls and godliness. Laodicea's self-serving, self-created standards in the name of love do not show love toward sinners, because the churchgoers in this city do not proclaim the good news of salvation in Jesus Christ. Caught up in itself and operating under its own bad judgment, the apostate church Laodicea is a poignant contrast to obedient Philadelphia.

Faithful Philadelphia is an active, engaged, believing church. Its faith is meaningful and it desires to pour everything into following Jesus with its heart, mind, strength, and soul. Philadelphian Christianity is not about being perfect in ourselves. It's about acknowledging our imperfection. Most importantly, it's about letting Jesus Christ be perfect for us. Philadelphian Christianity finds its fruit, rest, and joy in recognizing Jesus for who he is and delighting in that recognition.

The need to recognize and acknowledge Jesus as the Christ evokes our other level of application for these letters: the level of personal application. Each letter is written for a place, time, group, and person. That person is you, as much as it was any ancient Philadelphian. That person is each of us, individually. Jesus is speaking to you and me in this letter. Do we have the spiritual ears to hear what the Lord is saying? Isa 55 details his call to us:

> Ho, every one that thirsteth, come ye to the waters, and he that hath no money; come ye, buy, and eat; yea, come, buy wine and milk without money and without price. Wherefore do ye spend money for that which is not bread? and your labour for that which satisfieth not? hearken diligently unto me, and eat ye that which is good, and let your soul delight itself in fatness. Incline your ear, and come unto me: hear, and your soul shall live; and I will make an everlasting covenant with you, even the sure mercies of David. (vv. 1–3)

You do not have to be holy in order to call upon Jesus, nor do you have to purchase your own salvation. The Lord is offering you spiritual food and drink. He is the Bread of Life and the Living Water. You only have to come and ask for him to save you. Isa 55:3 is telling you to come, hear, and receive eternal life for your soul. If you do, your sins will be forgiven, and you will receive the benefit of the everlasting covenant of reconciliation with God. Delighting in God's mercies, you can live forever in his kingdom with him.

EPILOGUE

All it takes is the willingness to let your ears hear what he has to say. Jesus Christ is speaking to you. Will you hear him? That question can start any willing heart on the road to Philadelphia.

In itself, the letter to the Philadelphians contains more than enough teachings to last for a lifetime of practical spiritual application. Philadelphian Christianity emphasizes a full, humble relationship with Jesus. It is overwhelming in its scope. Nonetheless, the humility of Christianity always urges us to realize that we do have an overwhelming need to rely on God for everything in all circumstances. By meditating on the Bible with all that we have, doing our best to honor God and to make one right decision at a time, we can live a life of spiritual abundance with impact for the future with our precious Lord. Insofar as the entire Bible details a healthy relationship with Jesus Christ, the entire Bible is actually one long letter to the church of Philadelphia.

The letter in Rev 3 highlights an everyday faithfulness that operates in spite of how we see ourselves or what we could ever hope to achieve. The Philadelphians are recognized for their perseverance through the daily grind and in the bigger picture of missions. They are not all missionaries to foreign countries. Living in a gateway city between the East and West, the Philadelphians are only being asked to take advantage of the opportunities they already have. Faithfulness wherever they are and with whatever they are doing is what Jesus approves. Motivated by love for Jesus and the desire to serve God, such faithfulness involves acting in good stewardship with decisions and doctrines, holding fast to the content of the Bible in its own context, calling sin what it is and speaking the truth in love, and seeking to honor the Lord by pursuing what he says is right and good. "And be not conformed to this world: but be ye transformed by the renewing of your mind," reads Rom 12, "that ye may prove what is that good, and acceptable, and perfect, will of God" (v. 2).

We, too, are always living in what we might call a gateway city. Every day as we go about our daily chores and duties, we are abiding in a "country" on the cusp of eternity. Our temporary world is a temporary home for every human soul, but we are right here on the gateway between today and forever. Earth has and is a threshold on its own. Everyone has a permanent destination on the other side of death or Jesus' return. We are always in the place of the Philadelphian, living in a place where worlds meet and cultures collide. Eternity is reaching out even today to those who will accept Jesus and have a glorious future. Anyone willing can begin a relationship with Jesus Christ and begin living in eternal life right now. Salvation of the soul begins here! Condemnation of the soul begins here, as well, because life in this world is the "country" and "city" where eternal choices are made.

You may not be a formal preacher or official foreign missionary, but you are a person with everyday decisions, circumstances you can and cannot help, and a sphere of influence. You affect others by your responses to your situation, by your lifestyle choices, by your words and deeds. In many regards, you are in a position similar to that of the Philadelphian Christians. Jesus wants your faithfulness. He wants mine. Our faithful service and love for him is found in giving him our lives on an ongoing basis of "always" and "forever": living one minute and making one decision at a time, as the Philadelphians did, being aware that those minutes and decisions matter for a million years from now. Today carries eternal weight.

According to Jesus, the Philadelphians are not wrapped up in anxiety about whether or not the world agrees with them. The synagogue of Satan obviously condemned them. The Philadelphians only had a little strength left because they were having to endure. The patience Christ mentions was not won by attaining to any worldly accolades. Philadelphians had to be intentional and invested. Characteristically, these are people with their eyes fixed firmly on eternity. They watch for open doors from God himself. They watch for a deliverance through Jesus Christ. These are people focused on the eternal life as *life*—as dynamic engagement that entails thinking, feeling, focusing, moving forward. First John 2 describes them and sets them apart from the people of the world.

> And hereby we do know that we know him, if we keep his commandments. He that saith, I know him, and keepeth not his commandments, is a liar, and the truth is not in him. But whoso keepeth his word, in him verily is the love of God perfected: hereby know we that we are in him. (vv. 3–5)

First John further draws a clear distinction between the will of the world and the will of God:

> Love not the world, neither the things that are in the world. If any man love the world, the love of the Father is not in him. For all that is in the world, the lust of the flesh, and the lust of the eyes, and the pride of life, is not of the Father, but is of the world. And the world passeth away, and the lust thereof: but he that doeth the will of God abideth for ever. (2:15–17)

EPILOGUE

The opposition between eternal outcomes could not be plainer. Philadelphian Christianity finds the source of its strength and opportunity in Jesus alone. It recognizes that love for one another is the result of love for God and keeping his commands for every day. It dwells on the spirit of God's law, rather than pretending that it is perfect enough to keep the letter of the law (2 Cor 3:6). It prizes the teachings of God, rather than pretending that it can redefine good and evil for itself.

In summary, as we've seen, the Rev 3 letter to Philadelphia testifies to the state of the Philadelphian Christian's heart as a heart after Jesus. This heart allows God to be its leader. It draws near to him (Jas 4:8). It trusts in him in times of trouble and rests on his unrelenting goodness, unchanging faithfulness, and unending mercy (Ps 34:9–10). It goes to him and his Word for standards of good and evil (Ps 119:2, 16, 66; 2 Tim 3:16–17). Jesus is its heartbeat and its lifeblood.

There's so much more to say in the wealth of Scripture, and it seems truly overwhelming to us as individuals. The Philadelphian Christian's heart meets and takes God on God's own unconditional terms without attempting to negotiate its total surrender to him. It observes scriptural content in scriptural context without trying to redefine what the Lord says and how or why he says it. It seeks humility, teachability, and maturity in alignment with God's transforming, all-consuming Word. It condemns sin but commends the sinless Savior, proclaiming the essential message of salvation and grace to all who will ear.

Moreover, the Philadelphian Christian's heart is an expectant one. It lives joyfully in abundance and anticipation. It loves tenaciously, with patience and perseverance. It has a new Jerusalem passport in hand as it eagerly scans the clouds for the coming Author of salvation. The Philadelphian Christian's heart has eyes on the skies, watching for the Lord every second, and doing its best to make the seconds count (Eph 5:15–21).

Thankfully, Scripture constantly reminds us that Philadelphian Christianity does not define or depend on itself. When the Philadelphian Christian's spirit fails, it relies on Jesus just the same. It steadfastly waits for Jesus to come for his Bride (Matt 24:42, 25:13). It finds its blessed hope in Jesus, whatever may come (Titus 2:14).

Wow, you might be saying. I will never be enough to be like that. I can never measure up to those qualities. These are such tall orders. The Philadelphian Christians must have been superhuman.

EPILOGUE

It's absolutely accurate to say that none of us can measure up to these qualities of holiness, truth, faithfulness, and more. By God's grace, however, you and I do not have to be Philadelphian Christians on our own. We must remember that Jesus' words to the church demonstrate that Philadelphian Christianity is not meant for a spiritually "tall" people, but for spiritually "small" individuals. Philadelphian Christians were first and foremost reminded of their relationship with Jesus. He is the Holy One who is perfect. The Philadelphian church is not perfect, and its people would likely have been the first to say so.

Philadelphian Christianity is not meant for a spiritually "tall" and "great" human being, but for the tall and great God who uses little and imperfect human hearts. He asks for us to be willing to abide in him and to let us love him by letting him change us from the inside out. In this book's chapters and their accompanying reflection questions, we've considered practical steps that can help in fostering that transformative relationship. These steps include shaping habits such as studying Scripture by meditating on it, writing verses on notecards or posting them in places where we encounter them throughout the day, and setting goals to read through the Bible within a certain timeframe. Other steps are sharing wholesome Christian fellowship, singing hymns and worship songs that praise the Lord, and spending time in prayer. Still other steps might require us to forego worldly habits and guilty pleasures that pull us away from what is good and true (Phil 4:8–9). For us Philadelphian-Christian-wannabes, the continuous task is to take and internalize the truth of Jesus Christ as we seek an ever healthier, more fruitful connection to him. This is what life is all about, as the Bible reaffirms on every page. Our relationship with Jesus is the most important open door that he has opened. No one can shut this door.

All of the traits of Philadelphian Christianity are like threads in a brilliant, beautiful tapestry. Delightful, daunting, promising, and pragmatic, they appear throughout Scripture, and intertwine neatly in a growing, life-changing, and amazing personal relationship with Jesus. A fundamental passage weaving together these qualities is John 15. Here, Jesus speaks to the disciples shortly before he goes to the cross for our sins.

> Now ye are clean through the word which I have spoken unto you. Abide in me, and I in you. As the branch cannot bear fruit of itself, except it abide in the vine; no more can ye, except ye abide in me. I am the vine, ye are the branches: He that abideth in me,

EPILOGUE

> and I in him, the same bringeth forth much fruit: for without me ye can do nothing. (vv. 3–5)
>
> Herein is my Father glorified, that ye bear much fruit; so shall ye be my disciples. As the Father hath loved me, so have I loved you: continue ye in my love. If ye keep my commandments, ye shall abide in my love; even as I have kept my Father's commandments, and abide in his love. These things have I spoken unto you, that my joy might remain in you, and that your joy might be full. This is my commandment, That ye love one another, as I have loved you. (vv. 8–12)
>
> Henceforth I call you not servants; for the servant knoweth not what his lord doeth: but I have called you friends; for all things that I have heard of my Father I have made known unto you. Ye have not chosen me, but I have chosen you, and ordained you, that ye should go and bring forth fruit, and that your fruit should remain: that whatsoever ye shall ask of the Father in my name, he may give it you. These things I command you, that ye love one another. (vv. 15–17)
>
> Because ye are not of the world, but I have chosen you out of the world, therefore the world hateth you. Remember the word that I said unto you, The servant is not greater than his lord. (vv. 19b–20a)

These comforting verses start with the declaration that we are made clean through Christ alone (v. 3). Jesus is the bedrock for our faith. He makes us clean and sanctifies us in his holiness. As he told the Philadelphians, he is the Holy One.

From there, we are told to do our best to abide, remember, and watch. In doing so, since our focus will be on God, we will bear greater fruit than we could dream. His forgiveness is bigger than all of our fears and failures. For those of us seeking to be Philadelphian Christians, Jesus' words are reassuring as well as instructive. It's even more wonderful to recall that Jesus begins John 15 with an equally reassuring statement: "I am the true vine, and my Father is the husbandman" (v. 1). Christ points us to who he is from the very beginning. Our faith and fruit start and end with Jesus.

The teachings of Jesus Christ as Lord and Savior are teachings for an active, engaged faith that commits failures and successes to him. Philadelphian Christianity rests in the love of Christ. Following these teachings entails working to change and form everyday habits as well as thought patterns. One of the most important aspects of striving to follow Jesus is engaging our minds in discipleship through reason and memory. We remember that God has cleansed us and that we cannot and do not save ourselves. Philadelphian Christianity remembers that God is holy and that we are not. We can base everything on the purity of Jesus, as the Philadelphians did. Again, as Jesus says in John 15:3, "Now ye are clean through the word which I have spoken unto you."

Generally speaking, Philadelphian Christianity is a faith that remembers. Our faith grows as we remember what the Lord has done for us and others, writing down memories as "monuments" or speaking in testimony of his goodness. Celebrating the Lord's faithfulness and resting in him will result in an increased eagerness to be with him. As we celebrate who he is, we can celebrate the promise that he is returning at any time. He is faithful today as he has always been faithful in the past. He will be faithful in the future as he has always been. The Philadelphians were reminded of who Jesus was from the outset of his letter to them. They were asked to remember and urged to abide in that remembrance. Dwelling on God's eternal promises, Philadelphian Christianity anticipates eternity with Christ as something that is set in stone. Thus, it preemptively fosters "memories" of our future with Jesus through constant memories of Christ's faithfulness in the past and present.

In Rev 3, the instructions of "abide," "remember," and "watch" are right there to be held, cherished, and practiced. Like keys to the kingdom, they summarize the Philadelphian Christian's lifestyle as conveyed in Christ's letter to the church. The Philadelphian Christian lifestyle revolves around dwelling in Christ, remembering his character and his words, and watching for him to come at any time. The aspects of such wholesome, intentional faith are linked to intimacy with Jesus and anticipation of the imminency of his return, tied to a constant, intentional lifestyle of living today for tomorrow. Taken together, these elements are hallmarks of an obedient, vigilant fixation on Jesus Christ, the Savior—the Lord who is the daily delight and diligent object of the Philadelphian Christian's heart, mind, soul, and strength.

> Wherefore seeing we also are compassed about with so great a cloud of witnesses, let us lay aside every weight, and the sin which doth so easily beset us, and let us run with patience the race that is set before us, Looking unto Jesus the author and finisher of our faith; who for the joy that was set before him endured the cross, despising the shame, and is set down at the right hand of the throne of God. (Heb 12:1–2)

APPENDIX A

How to Be Saved

THE LETTER TO THE church of Philadelphia is an encouragement and instruction for Christians, but maybe that does not describe you personally. Do you know for certain that if you were to die right now, you would go to heaven to be with Jesus? The Bible states that there are only two eternal destinations. One is heaven, with Jesus Christ in eternal glory and joy (2 Cor 5:8, Phil 1:23, Rev 21–22). The other is hell, a place of utter darkness, torment, and separation from God (Matt 13:41–42, 49–50; 25:41, 46; Rev 20:11–15).

If you do not know Jesus Christ as your personal Lord and Savior, now is the time to be thinking about eternity. The steps to becoming a Christian are short and simple. If you are ready to turn to Jesus as your Lord and Savior and to form a relationship with him, read on. If you are not ready or if you doubt the truth of the Bible, then let the Rev 3 letter be a challenge to you. Investigate the Bible and what it says about who Jesus is. Examine its claims to truth. Countless apologetics resources exist in support of the Bible's accuracy and inspiration. There is more than reasonable cause to believe that the Bible is the inspired, infallible, and inerrant Word of God. The short bibliography at the end of this appendix provides a starting point for you, if you are willing. What do you have to lose? If the Bible is right, everything. Now really is the time, because it may be the only time you have. The Bible clearly says that there are no do-overs after death (Heb 9:27). You have this limited lifetime to either choose Jesus or reject him.

APPENDIX A: HOW TO BE SAVED

If you are ready to embrace Jesus, salvation is available to you right now. Understand that you are a sinner and that you have violated God's law in every little lie, malicious thought, petty theft, jealous wish, bitter word, or other trespass. Left to ourselves, we are condemned to hell by our own actions. God does not send anyone to hell. We send ourselves by committing unholy acts, saying unholy things, and thinking unholy thoughts. "For all have sinned, and come short of the glory of God" (Rom 3:23). We are all sinners.

The good news of the gospel is that, despite the undeniable fact that we are sinners, Jesus provides a way for us to be forgiven of our sins and to enjoy eternal life in heaven. He has atoned for your sins by dying on the cross and becoming a perfect sacrifice for you. By acknowledging that you are a sinner and asking him to forgive you, you can accept the atonement and receive new life in him. Romans 6:23 says, "For the wages of sin is death; but the gift of God is eternal life through Jesus Christ our Lord." Rom 10:9 tells us how to find forgiveness and eternal life in Jesus: "That if thou shalt confess with thy mouth the Lord Jesus, and shalt believe in thine heart that God hath raised him from the dead, thou shalt be saved."

The first step in being saved is knowing that you need to be saved. *Admit* that you are a sinner and that you must repent of your sins, rejecting them as evil and unholy. The next step is knowing that Jesus alone can save you and accepting him as Savior. *Believe* that he is Lord of all and that he has risen from the dead. *Call* upon Jesus with a simple prayer like this:

> Dear Jesus, I confess that I am a sinner and need You to save me. Please forgive me from my sins and take control of my life. Thank You for dying on the cross for me and rising again from the grave so that I could have eternal life in You. I give You my heart and soul, and ask You to become my Lord and Savior. In Jesus' name, amen.

If you prayed for salvation, you have just made the most crucial, wonderful decision of your life. Right now, the angels are rejoicing at the knowledge that your sins have been washed away (Luke 15:10). The Holy Spirit has entered your heart to claim you as God's own (Eph 1:13).

Take the next steps in your new life by obtaining a copy of the Holy Bible, God's Word. Read it every day and study it as a source of instruction, hope, and joy. Consider starting your reading in the Gospel of John, the fourth book in the New Testament. Seek out fellowship in a Bible-believing church that believes in Jesus Christ as the only way to heaven, as one with God the Father in the Holy Trinity of Father, Spirit, and Son, and as crucified, risen, and coming again; and that believes in the Holy Bible as the inspired, infallible, and inerrant Word of God and as the source of unchanging, absolute truth and morality. Pray with the assurance that God hears you. Grow in your faith by learning more about why the Bible is true and reliable. The bibliography below has more information to help you. Review the reflection questions in this book for more ideas on how to form good habits and focus your heart, mind, and soul on Jesus. Celebrate the certainty that you have a new life in Jesus and are guaranteed eternity in heaven. If you belong to Jesus, the best is yet to come!

> But as many as received him, to them gave he power to become the sons of God, even to them that believe on his name. (John 1:12)
>
> There is therefore now no condemnation to them which are in Christ Jesus, who walk not after the flesh, but after the Spirit. For the law of the Spirit of life in Christ Jesus hath made me free from the law of sin and death. (Rom 8:1–2)
>
> But thanks be to God, which giveth us the victory through our Lord Jesus Christ. (1 Cor 15:57)

More about the Bible: A Very Short Sample Bibliography

Ankerberg Theological Research Institute. *The John Ankerberg Show*. https://jashow.org.

Christian Apologetics and Research Ministry. https://carm.org.

Copan, Paul. *True for You, But Not for Me: Overcoming Objections to Christian Faith*. Bloomington, MN: Bethany House Publishers, 2009.

Craig, William Lane. *Reasonable Faith: Christian Truth and Apologetics*. Wheaton, IL: Crossway, 1994.

Geisler, Norman, and Frank Turek. *I Don't Have Enough Faith to Be an Atheist*. Wheaton, IL: Crossway, 2004.

Josh McDowell, a CRU Ministry. https://www.josh.org.

Lewis, C. S. *Mere Christianity*. New York: Harper Collins, 1952.

McDowell, Josh, and Sean McDowell. *Evidence That Demands a Verdict: Life-Changing Truth for a Skeptical World*. Nashville: Thomas Nelson, 2017.

Probe for Answers. Probe Ministries. https://probe.org.

Strobel, Lee. *The Case for Christ: A Journalist's Personal Investigation of the Evidence for Jesus*. Grand Rapids: Zondervan, 2016.

Wallace, J. Warner, and Jimmy Wallace. Cold-Case Christianity. https://coldcasechristianity.com.

Wilkinson, Bruce, and Kenneth Boa. *Talk Thru the Bible*. Nashville: Thomas Nelson, 1983.

APPENDIX B

Historical Philadelphia

As discussed in the introduction, historical Philadelphia was a famous city in ancient Asia Minor (38° 21′ 0″ N, 28° 31′ 0″ E[1]). Philadelphia was the city of "brotherly love," receiving its name from the mutual fraternal affection of two literal brothers. The word Philadelphia comes from two Greek word roots: φίλ- (*phil-*), "love," and ἀδελφ- (*adelph-*), "brotherly." The two brothers were Eumenes II and Attalus II. Living in the second century BC, they were members of the Attalid kingly dynasty in western Asia Minor. Their kingdom had its capital at Pergamon.

Pergamon was another city that will be familiar to readers of Revelation. Pergamon, also known as Pergamos or Pergamum, is the site of one of the other seven churches in Rev 2–3. The church of Pergamon is addressed by Jesus in Rev 2 (vv. 12–17). Unlike the church of Philadelphia, the church of Pergamon does not receive top marks from Christ. Pergamon is not an approved church. Jesus' concerns with Pergamon are quite serious. Reading through his letter, we find that the grave message to Pergamon introduces us to a world-bound church that needs to repent or face God's judgment. Philadelphia is a promising church with a glowing future. Pergamon is a compromising church with a grim future. The contrast is stark.

The kingdom of Pergamon was a wealthy Hellenistic state. It was a prosperous home for Philadelphia's founders, the two brothers. Pergamon's kingdom had grown out of territory belonging to one of Alexander

1. "Alaşehir."

the Great's generals. A renowned military genius from Macedonia, Alexander died abruptly at a young age. He left behind a vast empire. Without a clear line of succession, Alexander's generals fell into a heated power struggle. Their respective holdings developed into kingdoms, some of them stronger than others. Written centuries before Alexander the Great himself was even born, the prophetic chapter of Dan 11 provides astoundingly detailed and accurate information about these Hellenistic kingdoms and their dynasties. Philadelphia is one of many, many cities impacted by the events prophetically recorded in Dan 11.

Lasting from the early third to mid-second centuries BC, the Attalid kingdom based in Pergamon became a Roman holding in 133 BC. The transition to Roman power was relatively peaceful. Attalus III, the final king of Pergamon, was the son of our first Philadelphian brother, Eumenes II, and therefore the nephew of the second Philadelphian brother, Attalus II. Attalus III left no male heirs when he died. Upon his death, he willed the Attalid kingdom to the Roman Republic. In spite of an ensuing revolt and civil uprisings, the kingdom of Pergamon with all of its riches and resources soon became securely Roman. The former kingdom would remain ready and waiting to hear the gospel over a century later, as when we encounter them in Revelation.

Philadelphia shared in the wealth and fame of the Attalid kingdom of Pergamon. Philadelphia was always part of a wealthy area. Long before the Hellenistic kingdom of Pergamon existed, western Asia Minor was once the empire of Lydia. Lydia's reputation is intrinsically caught up with stories of gold, pomp, and power. If you've ever heard the proverb "rich as Croesus," then you've already heard of Lydia. Croesus was an extremely wealthy, influential king of Lydia. His personal story is actually more a story related to Sardis, another one of the seven churches in Rev 2–3. Nonetheless, the region of Philadelphia was also Lydian. Philadelphia's founding under the Attalids merely meant that the people in Philadelphia were associated with yet another wealthy dynasty after Lydia.

As a city, Philadelphia was a renowned center for trade. It was a cultural hub in its own right. Philadelphia was situated comfortably near to four of the other cities mentioned in Rev 2–3. Given that each of these other four cities was wealthy and important, Philadelphia benefited from and contributed to burgeoning trade in the area. Its volcanic soil made it perfect for planting healthy vineyards. Crops grew well in Philadelphia. The metaphor of the healthy soil is particularly meaningful for Philadelphia. In spiritual terms, the church in Philadelphia was an exceptionally healthy "vineyard." Physical crops prospered in the fertile soil of Philadelphia. Spiritual crops did, as well. Jesus Christ would have a healthy following in Philadelphia. There was useful soil in the region of this city, physically and spiritually.

Philadelphia had more to commend it. Originally, it was founded as a missionary city—not a missionary city for Christianity, mind you, at least, not at the beginning. Philadelphia was a missionary city for secular relationships, like commercial and industrial trades, and for cultural influences. With an ideal location for forging connections between the East and West, Philadelphia was a gateway city from one part of the world to the other. Traders could easily reach and pass through this city. Serving as the connection between Europe and Asia, Philadelphia was meant to spread Greek culture to the rest of the world. The city's mixed population bore witness to its success as a base for Hellenistic outreach.

For the ancients, Greek language and civilization came along with Greek gods and their worship. Philadelphia later wore the title "Little Athens" because the city contained so much pagan architecture by the sixth century AD. The original Greek city of Athens was famous for its architectural feats, especially its temples, and for its cult feasts. As Little Athens, Philadelphia earned similar esteem for architecture and pagan associations. It, too, became known for its temples and its dedication to false gods. Philadelphia's affiliation with paganism began early and continued in spite of the Christian influences in the city. As it continued to spread Greek culture, Philadelphia remained a thriving hub of Greek cults and civilization.

Despite its favorable location and kingly backing, secular Philadelphia was not without its own physical challenges. Its location in an earthquake-heavy region made it susceptible to damage. In AD 17, Philadelphia and its surrounding cities were ravaged by an intense earthquake that struck in the middle of the night. The Roman historian Pliny called it the "greatest earthquake in human memory."[2] Another historian, Tacitus, relates horrors recalled by eyewitnesses. He speaks of massive mountains sinking into the ground, plain land raised so that it towered into the sky, and fires blazing throughout the devastation.[3] In the wake of the extreme disaster, Philadelphia and its neighboring cities received tax relief and the honor of an official visit from a representative of the Roman Senate. The

2. Pliny, *Nat. Hist.* 2.86.200.
3. Tacitus, *Ann.* 2.47.

envoy's task was to assess the destruction and evaluate how the empire could best help rebuild the ruined cities.[4]

Philadelphia's vulnerability was known for years prior to this great Lydian earthquake. Not long before the first-century incident recorded by Pliny and Tacitus, the geographer Strabo writes of the frequent earthquake activity in the area. Strabo reports that the earthquakes were so common and severe that most of Philadelphia's population elected to live in the country. For the majority of Philadelphians, the choice reflected necessity. Earthquakes were such a fact of life that, for many, living outside the city hub was a matter of survival. City buildings were constantly suffering from tremors. The fields were safer. After all, buildings couldn't fall on you as easily if you didn't live around as many of them. Accordingly, "the majority of the people pass their lives as farmers in the country," Strabo writes, noting the productive soil enjoyed by the Philadelphian farming community.[5] He goes on to express admiration for those who braved city-living. "Nonetheless, we may marvel at the few [city-dwellers], that they are so fond of the place, though their dwellings are in a precarious position. One might wonder still more at those who founded the city."[6]

In the late first century AD, around the time when John was sending Jesus' letter to the Philadelphian church, Philadelphia continued to be a robust center of civilization and agriculture. It was known for its grapes and wine. Actually, Philadelphia almost suffered a grievous blow from the same Roman emperor who went to lengths to persecute John. Reigning from AD 81–96, Emperor Domitian is one of the emperors most associated with persecution of the early church. Domitian reportedly sought to kill John, failed, and eventually settled on sending the elderly apostle to die on the island of Patmos. Domitian's machinations against John and the gospel message didn't work, however. John received the letters and vision of Revelation while imprisoned on Patmos. Furthermore, John outlived Domitian, and legend has it that the apostle later returned to the city of Ephesus until his own death at a ripe old age.

The people of Philadelphia nearly felt the brunt of Domitian's harshness in connection with their local produce. In the early 90s, during a grain famine, Emperor Domitian ordered at least half of all vineyards in

---

4. As further detailed by Tacitus, *Ann.* 2.47; and mentioned by Suetonius, *Tib.* 48, and Strabo, 13.4.8.

5. Strabo, 13.4.10.

6. Strabo, 13.4.10.

Asia and other Roman provinces to be cut down. The biographer Suetonius says that Domitian believed fields were being neglected in favor of vineyards.[7] Another ancient writer, Philostratus, recounts that Domitian had a more political motive. According to Philostratus, Domitian believed that drinking wine would embolden the people of Asia to plot revolution against him.[8] It's also possible that Domitian was favoring Italy over Asia. For Philadelphia, a city intensely dependent on the production of wine and grapes, the edict would have been particularly severe. The Asian cities reportedly sent a desperate embassy to Domitian, hoping to convince him to show mercy. Thanks to a particularly persuasive ambassador, Domitian apparently yielded and recalled the decree.[9]

Over the centuries, Philadelphia persisted as a center for trade and culture. In the fifth and sixth centuries AD, almost five hundred years after Jesus' letter to the church, Philadelphia remained a flourishing crossroads. It continued its central mission as a gateway city. As such, Little Athens, a.k.a. Byzantine Philadelphia, retained its cult ties and its pagan rituals and architecture. The city still had other troubles, of course. In the eleventh century (AD 1074 and 1093–94), Seljuk Turks captured Philadelphia twice. Emperor Alexius I took it back in the First Crusade. In the twelfth century, more than one revolt against the Byzantine emperors commenced in Philadelphia.

As time passed, Philadelphia faced the growing threat of the Ottomans. While under constant attacks, the city refused to surrender and maintained as much of its independence as possible. Its defensible location worked in its favor, helping it to stay out of the hands of besieging armies. For generations, Philadelphia stayed virtually independent, although it was nominally part of the Byzantine Empire. It stood as a final holdout amidst Ottoman emirates. Philadelphia "displayed all the noble qualities of endurance, truth and steadfastness, which are attributed to it in the letter of St. John, amid the ever threatening danger of Turkish attack," writes Ramsay. He adds, "During the fourteenth century [Philadelphia] stood practically alone against the entire Turkish power as a free, self-governing Christian city amid a Turkish land."[10] In 1378, the struggling Byzantine Empire negotiated with the Turks and agreed to give Philadelphia to the Ottomans. Philadelphia fought the

7. Suetonius, *Dom.* 7.
8. Philostratus, *Lives of the Sophists* 520.
9. Philostratus, *Life of Apollonius* 6.42.
10. Ramsay, *Letters to the Seven Churches*, 400.

APPENDIX B: HISTORICAL PHILADELPHIA

concession and held out under a lengthy twelve-year siege. In 1390, at long last, Sultan Bayezid I commanded the subjugated co-emperors of Byzantium to help him take the city once and for all.

Philadelphia's defeat in 1390 marked a turning point in the history of Asia Minor. The city that had been a nominal outpost for Byzantium now lost its influence and independence. When Philadelphia fell, the Ottoman Empire officially asserted sovereignty over the entire region. In the early 1400s, the brutal Turco-Mongol emperor Timur (Tamerlane) defeated Bayezid I and seized Philadelphia. Decades later, the Ottomans retook the territory. Here, Philadelphia would seem to present another lesson for the modern Christian. Though a comparatively tiny outpost, Philadelphia represented a hope for freedom as long as the city held out and strove to cling to its roots. For many years, Philadelphia tried to stand fast. It staved off Ottoman claims to the entire area. Philadelphia is an object lesson: one small city, like one small individual, can make a vast difference in history.

By the 1800s, Philadelphia's population was largely Muslim. Greek forces held Philadelphia from 1920 to 1922 during the Greco-Turkish War; and in 1922, in the ongoing conflict, the city was almost razed by fire. War, the fire, and the people's rush to escape had dire results for old Philadelphia. One source estimates that the city's population was reduced from thirty-eight thousand people to six thousand.[11]

How did Philadelphia fare spiritually over the passing centuries? Although outnumbered, Christians endured in the city. Jesus' encouraging letter in Rev 3 did not free the believers there from persecution. In AD 156, sixty years or so after Christ's letter, eleven Christians from Philadelphia were martyred alongside Polycarp of Smyrna.[12] In more recent times, Turkish believers are still being eradicated, exiled, and persecuted in other ways. Of the entire country of Turkey, less than 0.2 percent of the Turkish population in 2022 identified as either Christian or otherwise non-Muslim.[13]

Located in modern Turkey's Manisa Province, the city of Philadelphia is today known as Alaşehir. Archaeological ruins of the ancient site are visible to this day. In fact, three of the stone pillars of the Byzantine-era Church of St. John the Theologian are among the city's most prominent archaeological remains.[14] Known for its raisins, fruits, and mineral

---

11. Atala and Salman, "Methodology," 40.
12. *Martyrdom of Polycarp*, 19.1.
13. See Office of International Religious Freedom, "2022 Report," sec. 2, para. 68.
14. For more, see Fant and Reddish, *Guide to Biblical Sites*, 300–302.

waters, among other things, the city of Alaşehir has continued to grow in the early twenty-first century. In 2022, Alaşehir had an estimated population of over fifty-seven thousand people.[15] Compare this with the mere six thousand who reportedly lived there after the Greco-Turkish War and associated dangers of 1922!

Philadelphia has come a long way from its beginnings millennia ago, but its most enduring historical legacy for the Christian is truly captured in the various elements of Christ's letter to the church there. Philadelphia was in a gateway location where East and West meet, mirroring the meeting of all peoples who are willing to come to Christ. In the Church, there is no East or West, no Jew or Greek, no slave or free, no male or female. "For as many of you as have been baptized into Christ have put on Christ" (Gal 3:27). Anyone can call upon Jesus Christ and find salvation in him (Eph 2:13–18). Secular Philadelphia, the city of Asia Minor, was built for the purpose of missions and outreach. Spiritual Philadelphia, the church based in the city, was a powerhouse of evangelism. Through Rev 3, Philadelphia is still spiritually serving the purpose of missions and outreach to us today.

Philadelphia was a city of access, prosperity and opportunity, and independence. It had standards and held to them uncompromisingly, as evident in the fact that it stood strong against generations of Ottoman encroachment. Investing in commerce and agriculture at key times and from a key location, Philadelphia reaped benefits for its original kings and its citizens across time. As we discover in Jesus' letter, investment in growth and proper opportunities is another important aspect of the healthy Philadelphian Christian mindset. Jesus speaks of crops, seeds, and other agricultural terms in numerous comparisons with Christian life. John 15 opens with a profound agricultural statement: "I am the true vine, and my Father is the husbandman" (v. 1). The Philadelphians know about growth and fruit-bearing in their walk with Christ, and it shows in what he tells them about their future.

We may not come to the book of Revelation expecting a history lesson. Revelation seems so much more connected to the future and end times, and for that reason alone, many Christians are too reluctant to read it. Revelation does have much to say about the future and events leading up to Jesus' return in the completed Second Coming. The world will one day enter into an intense time of God's judgment upon its habitants. Jesus

---

15. "Alaşehir in Alaşehir (Manisa)."

APPENDIX B: HISTORICAL PHILADELPHIA

describes this time as "great tribulation, such as was not since the beginning of the world to this time, no, nor ever shall be" (Matt 24:21b).

But recognizing Revelation as a book of very real future events should not cause us to separate the book from its roots in the past. We cannot ignore the historicity of the churches, any more than we should be neglecting what the book means for us today and tomorrow. More than ever, we should be paying rapt attention. The Bible warns that we are right now living in the future and in the end times (as stated in 1 John 2:18 or Heb 1:2, for example).

All in all, Revelation is built on a historical foundation, because Scripture is accurate and true. The events of the Bible directly reflect things that really happened and look ahead to other things that really will happen. Revelation 2 and 3 were written to churches that really existed. As were the rest of the letters in the Bible, these letters were addressed to actual people. Their very real existence is a vital reason for grounding ourselves in the history of Philadelphia as we open to Rev 3. The more we know about historical Philadelphia, the more sense we can make of the special little allusions and comments that Jesus makes to the historical people who lived and died in this city. The historicity of Philadelphia is a wonderful fact for us to remember. The first recipients of the Philadelphian letter were every bit as real and alive as we are today. Christ's letter to them has been carefully preserved for our sakes, as well, as Jesus commanded for it to be.

Bibliography

"Alaşehir." GeoHack. Last updated July 9, 2024. https://geohack.toolforge.org/geohack.php?pagename=Alaşehir&params=38_21_N_28_31_E_region:TR_type:adm1st_dim:100000.

"Alaşehir in Alaşehir (Manisa)." City Population, Dec. 31, 2022. https://citypopulation.de/en/turkey/manisa/alaşehir/161__alaşehir/.

Atala, Zeren Önsel, and S. Yildiz Salman. "A Methodology for the Conservation of Small Anatolian Cities Planned between 1920 and 1960." In *Heritage Architecture Studies*, edited by Víctor Echarri Iribarren and C. A. Brebbia, 37–47. Southampton, UK: WIT, 2018.

"The Controversy over the Name of Yeshua." Bibles for Israel and the Messianic Bible Project. https://free.messianicbible.com/feature/the-controversy-over-the-name-of-yeshua/.

Fant, Clyde E., and Mitchell G. Reddish. *A Guide to Biblical Sites in Greece and Turkey*. New York: Oxford University Press, 2003.

Fruchtenbaum, Arnold. *The Feasts and Fasts of Israel: Their Historic and Prophetic Significance*. San Antonio: Ariel Ministries, 2019.

Got Questions. "What Is the Significance of Pomegranates in the Bible?" Last updated Jan. 4, 2022. https://www.gotquestions.org/pomegranates-in-the-Bible.html.

Hershey, Doug. "Yeshua: The Meaning of the Hebrew Name of Jesus." FIRM, Dec. 22, 2015. https://firmisrael.org/learn/who-is-yeshua-meaning-of-hebrew-name-jesus/.

Liddell, Henry George, et al., eds. *A Greek–English Lexicon*. 9th ed. Oxford: Clarendon, 1940.

"No One Else Brings Salvation but Yeshua." Bibles for Israel and the Messianic Bible Project. https://free.messianicbible.com/feature/one-else-brings-salvation-yeshua/.

Office of International Religious Freedom. "2022 Report on International Religious Freedom: Turkey (Türkiye)." U.S. Department of State. https://www.state.gov/reports/2022-report-on-international-religious-freedom/turkey/.

Orr, James, ed. *International Standard Bible Encyclopedia*. Chicago: Howard-Severance, 1915.

Pember, G. H. *Earth's Earliest Ages and Their Connection with Modern Spiritualism and Theosophy*. 5th ed. London: Hodder and Stoughton, 1889.

BIBLIOGRAPHY

———. *The Great Prophecies concerning the Gentiles, the Jews, and the Church of God.* London: Hodder and Stoughton, 1881.

Powell, Mark Allen. *HarperCollins Bible Dictionary.* Abridged ed. San Francisco: HarperOne, 2009. https://www.bibleodyssey.org/glossary. Accessed using Bible Odyssey.

Ramsay, William M. *The Letters to the Seven Churches of Asia and Their Place in the Plan of the Apocalypse.* London: Hodder and Stoughton, 1904.

Strong, James. *Strong's Exhaustive Concordance of the Bible.* 1890. https://biblehub.com/. Accessed using Bible Hub.

Thayer, Joseph Henry. *A Greek-English Lexicon of the New Testament: Being Grimm's Wilke's Clavis Novi Testamenti.* New York: American Book, 1889.

Treybig, David. "Smyrna." Life, Hope & Truth. https://lifehopeandtruth.com/prophecy/revelation/seven-churches-of-revelation/smyrna/.

Watkins, Calvert, ed. *The American Heritage Dictionary of Indo-European Roots.* 3rd ed. Boston: Houghton Mifflin Harcourt, 2011.

Subject Index

Abraham, 77, 83, 87
absolute truth, 6, 16, 30–31, 35, 37–38, 133
Adam, 10, 39n2, 72, 77
age of grace, 77, 85
agriculture, 138, 141. *See also* vineyard(s)
Agrippa
    Herod Agrippa II, in the book of Acts, 102–3
    Marcus (Vipsanius) Agrippa, and the Pantheon, 118
Alaşehir, 140–41
Alexander the Great, 135–36
angel(s), 39, 58, 73, 91, 99, 132
anti-Semitism, condemned, 82
Antichrist, 35, 96
Antipas, 12
apologetics, 132–33
apostasy, xx, 3, 5, 30, 71–74, 94–96, 113, 124
    of ancient Israel, 16
apostolic age, 3, 81, 92, 98
    and awareness of prophecy, 101–3, 111
archaeology, 89, 140
Attalus II, xv–xvi, 135–36

Baal Peor, 12
Balaam, 12
Beatitudes, 61, 93
Berean(s), 67–69

Bible, nature of. *See also* inspiration of Scripture, inerrancy, infallibility, 6–7, 16, 30, 37, 44, 68–69, 87, 92, 101, 103, 109, 125, 131, 133, 142
birth of Jesus, xvi, 35, 39, 45
Boaz, 114, 116–17
Body of Christ, xx, 4–5, 19, 51, 61, 63, 84–86, 88, 110, 115, 123
Branch, as a messianic title, 73
bride. *See* wedding
Bride of Christ, as a title for the Church, 4, 83, 91–92, 97, 104, 110, 119, 127
bronze, 117
    of the temple pillars, 113–14, 116
brotherly love
    and Philadelphia's name, xvi, 59, 135
    biblically defined, 61, 63, 66, 87
Byzantium, 139–40

Church Invisible, 4–6, 19, 97, 110
Church Visible, 4–6, 19, 123
circumcision, 66
clean and unclean animals, 24–25
confession
    and the Philadelphian church, 81
    of Christ as Lord, 71, 75–77, 132
    of sins, 27, 132
Constantine, 3
contest, the Christian life as, 65–66, 69
Croesus, 15, 136

SUBJECT INDEX

crucifixion, of Christ, 10, 32, 58, 98, 133
curse of sin and death. *See also* sin(s), 26, 39, 77–78, 119, 121

David, 38–47, 54, 58, 102, 113, 115, 124
demon(s), 12, 32, 74–75
denial
  of Christ, 11, 27, 30, 32, 55, 70–74, 76–78, 81–82, 89, 94
  of Christians' legitimacy (by synagogue of Satan), 83
  of worldliness, 91
devil. *See* Satan
dianoia, 64
disciple(s). *See* apostolic age, 29, 33, 34, 36, 41–42, 50, 58, 65, 70, 98, 101–4, 106, 111, 115, 128
discipleship, 36, 129–30
doctrine, xix, 5, 7, 10, 12–13, 36, 43, 70, 83, 85–86, 94–95, 98, 103, 125
Domitian, 138–39
door(s)
  and keys, 38, 47, 55, 58
  and salvation, 46–50, 52, 68
  as opportunities, 47, 49–56, 58–60, 68, 80, 126, 128

early church. *See also* apostolic age, 3, 5, 18, 51, 81, 92, 98, 101–3, 105, 107, 111, 138
earthquake(s), 15, 22, 89, 112–13, 120, 137–38
East, 15, 18, 84, 137, 141
  of Philadelphia as a gateway to. *See* gateway
Eliakim, 41–43, 46–47
end times, 71, 92, 94–96, 98, 141–42
endurance (patience), 10, 13, 64, 88, 89–91, 94, 96, 106, 116, 126–27, 130, 139
  and the historical city of Philadelphia, 139–40
Ephesus, xvi, 2–3, 9–10, 13, 18, 52, 92, 123, 138
eschatology. *See also* end times, 95, 98
Eumenes II, xv–xvi, 135–36
Eusebius, 82

evangelism, 3, 21, 36, 48–49, 66, 84–85, 93, 96–97, 101–2, 105, 109, 141
Eve, 10, 37, 39n2, 72, 77

faith, xix, 2, 13–14, 18, 26, 44, 47, 52, 55, 59, 62–68, 70–71, 75–77, 79, 82–83, 85, 87, 89–91, 94, 101, 107, 110, 115–16, 119, 124, 129, 130, 133
fall of man. *See* sin(s), 10, 39, 71
feast(s)
  of Israel, 82, 87, 101
  pagan (of cults), 137
fellowship, 3, 9–10, 107, 110–11, 115–16, 121, 128, 132
First Coming, 98, 104
First Temple, 23, 113–17, 122

gateway, Philadelphia as a, 15, 18, 49–50, 52, 84, 125, 137, 139, 141
Great Tribulation, 14, 93, 95, 142
groom. *See* wedding

hallelujah, 56–57
heaven
  and kingdom of, xx, 7, 16, 18, 26–27, 39, 44, 46–48, 56, 58, 65–67, 71–75, 91, 98–99, 101, 103–4, 110, 112, 115, 117, 119–21, 131–33
  of new heaven(s) and new earth, 10, 78, 119
hell, xix, 11, 47, 70, 75, 131–32
Hellenism, and Greek culture, 135–37
Hilkiah, 41–42
homologeō. *See* confession, 76
humility, 29, 36, 44–45, 58–59, 64, 68, 74, 86–87, 107, 125, 127
hypomonē. *See* endurance, 90

Ignatius, 83n2
imminency, 65, 98, 105, 111, 130
inerrancy, 7, 131, 133
infallibility, 131, 133
inscription(s), promised for the Philadelphian overcomer, 118–20
inspiration of Scripture, 6–7, 102, 109, 131, 133

SUBJECT INDEX

intentionality. *See also dianoia*, xx, 40, 61, 64–67, 103, 110–11, 126, 130
investment, eternal, 60, 66, 100, 126, 141
ischus, 65
Israel, 12–13, 16, 22, 24, 26, 28, 32, 39, 63, 81, 83–87
    kingdom of, 13, 39–40

Jachin, 114, 116–17
Jerusalem, 39n2, 40–41, 84, 87, 101, 113–15
Jezebel, 13–14
Job, 90
John the apostle, xvi, 2, 18, 27, 90, 95, 110, 116, 132, 138–39
    and the Church of St. John the Theologian, in Philadelphia, 140
John the Baptist, 33–35, 65
Joshua, and Yeshua, 73, 79
Judah, kingdom of, 40–41
judgment. *See also* Tribulation, Second Coming, 12–14, 32, 34, 40–41, 56, 72, 85, 92–93, 99, 105, 121, 135, 141
    of the people. *See* Laodicea, 16, 124

kathēkonta, 72
key(s), 38–47, 55, 58, 115
King of kings, 14, 39, 41, 46, 75, 121
kingdom(s), 38–40, 47, 98
    of Alexander the Great's successors, 136
    of heaven. *See also* heaven, 17, 33, 39–40, 45–47, 52, 103, 106, 115, 124, 130
    of Israel and Judah, 40
    of Pergamon, 135–36

Laodicea, xvi, 3, 5, 16–18, 94–96, 123–24
last days. *See* end times, 3, 30–31, 93–96, 105, 123
law, 7, 12, 25, 33–34, 63, 82, 84, 101, 103, 127, 132
    and the prophets, 33–34, 82, 103
    of the Spirit of life, 133
    referring to the one law in Eden, 39n2

levels of interpretation and application, 1–8, 18, 110, 124
light, of Christ, xx, 43–44, 90, 109–10
lilies, 113, 117
Little Athens, Philadelphia as, 137, 139
love. *See also* brotherly love, xvi, xix, 17, 28, 43, 45, 50, 59–64, 66, 71, 80–84, 86–87, 89, 92, 101, 105–7, 109–10, 115, 117, 120, 125–29, 135
    and sinfulness. *See also* Laodicea, 74, 124
    of Christ, as reflected in marriage (and in the Song of Solomon), 4, 117
    of lost love of Ephesus, 3, 10
Lydia, 15, 120, 136, 138

Marcus Agrippa. *See* Agrippa
marriage. *See also* wedding, Bride, 4, 104
    of Israel and Moab at Baal Peor, 12
    of King Ahab and Queen Jezebel, 14
    of Pergamon and the world, 3
maturity, spiritual, 109, 127
martyrdom, 5, 12, 70, 140
memory, of God's faithfulness, 130
Messiah, 16–17, 26, 33–36, 39–40, 42, 44, 45–46, 54, 59, 73, 79, 81, 84–85, 89, 101, 103, 112, 119
messianic kingdom, 39–40, 73, 98
    and Christ's reign from Jerusalem, 41, 84, 87
messianic prophecy, 16, 33–35, 37, 39, 46, 73, 102–4, 119
mimētai, 42
missionary. *See* missions
    referring to Philadelphia as a secular missionary city, 15, 52, 137, 139, 141
missionary age, 3, 93
missions, 3, 5, 15, 36, 50–52, 54–55, 58, 84, 87, 90, 93, 96, 107, 109, 125–26, 141
Mosaic law. *See also* law, 7, 25, 84, 101, 103
Moses, 22, 35, 103
myrrh, 11

SUBJECT INDEX

Nero, 107
new Jerusalem, 112, 116, 118–20, 127
New Testament saints. *See* saint(s), 119

Old Testament saints. *See* saint(s), 79, 119

pagan(ism), 12, 14, 30, 32, 137, 139
Pantheon, 118
parable(s)
 of the rich man, 41
 of the sower and seed, 89, 96
 of the talents, 43
Passover, 81
Paul, 4, 11, 21, 43–44, 52, 55–57, 59–61, 65–66, 69, 84–85, 87, 91, 93–94, 98–100, 102–4, 106, 108–9
peace. *See* shalom, 67, 84, 120–21
 as reconciliation with God, 67, 71, 83–84
Pember, G. H., 61, 100
Pentecost, 101
Pergamon (Pergamos, Pergamum), xv–xvi, 3, 11–13, 18, 92, 123, 135–36
Pergamon Altar, 11
persecution, 3, 10–11, 15, 18, 57, 70–71, 78, 80–82, 89, 92–94, 96, 107–8, 138, 140
Peter, 6, 23–24, 26, 58, 65, 73, 102–4, 106, 115
petra, 115
petros, 115
Philostratus, 139
Pliny (the Elder), 137–38
Polycarp, 140
pomegranates, 113, 117
Pontius Pilate, 32–33, 35–36
praos, 59
priest(s)
 and priesthood, 73, 84, 87
 referring to pagan priests and priestcraft, 13
prophecy. *See also* end times, law and the prophets, messianic prophecy, xvii, xix, 6, 8, 16, 29, 31–35, 37, 39–40, 42, 46, 49, 65, 71, 73, 82, 85, 93–96, 98, 100–104, 113, 117, 136

 of Balaam the prophet. *See* Balaam, 12
 of Jezebel the prophetess in Thyatira. *See* Jezebel, 13
 of the Lord's prophets, 23, 33–34, 40, 73, 82, 93–94, 102
 on the study of, 100–103
Proto-Indo-European (word roots), 21, 31, 74
psychē, 64

Ramsay, William, 89, 121, 139
Rapture, and Christ's coming any minute. *See also* imminency, 65, 91–93, 95–99, 104–5, 108, 111, 119, 127, 133
replacement theology, and concept of replacing the ethnic Jews, 81, 85, 87
reconciliation with God. *See* peace, 67, 77, 124
relative truth, 30–31, 37
resurrection
 of believers, 60, 91
 of Christ, 10, 35, 102, 119, 132–33
revival, xx, 3
 of Israel, 84
rewards, eternal, xvii, 9, 11, 76–77, 94, 106, 113, 117
 in the parable of the talents, 43
Rome, and Empire of, 2–3, 18, 52, 103, 118, 120, 136–39

saint(s), 11, 15, 26, 43, 66, 79, 95, 119
 across the ages. *See* Old Testament saints, New Testament saints, Tribulation saints
 and the meaning of, 26
salvation, xix, 23, 34, 44, 47–52, 66, 72–79, 81–82, 85, 89, 91, 102, 107, 110, 119, 124, 126–27, 132, 141
 and being saved, xviii, 21, 23, 28, 46, 48–49, 61, 66–67, 73, 75–77, 83–86, 90, 92, 95, 100, 114, 117, 119–20, 132
 and the meaning of, 74
 and the name of Jesus. *See* Yeshua, 73, 77–79, 107

sanctification, 23, 25–26, 28, 129
Sardis, xvi, 14–16, 18, 123, 136
Second Coming, 40, 65, 95, 98–99, 104, 121, 133, 141
 of Christ's coming for His Bride, prior to the Revelation coming. *See* Rapture
Second Temple, 98
Seventieth Week, 93
Satan, xix, 10–12, 30, 37, 57, 66, 70, 74–75, 77, 80–83, 86–88, 90, 107, 126
 synagogue of. *See* synagogue of Satan
shalom, 67
Shebna, 40–43, 47
sin(s), xix–xx, 4, 10, 17, 21, 23, 25–28, 33, 37, 39–41, 48, 56, 62, 64, 70, 72–75, 77–79, 82, 87, 92, 105, 114, 119–21, 124–25, 127–28, 130, 132–33
Sinai, Mt., 22
Smyrna, xvi, xx, 3, 10–11, 80–83, 86–87, 90–92, 123, 140
Solomon, 113–15, 117
sower, the parable of. *See* parable(s)
stewardship, 40–49, 59, 62, 86, 125
Strabo, 138
supersessionism. *See* replacement theology, 85
sword of the Spirit, 11, 13
 referring to the Word, 103
synagogue(s), 11, 87, 102
 referring to synagogue(s) of Satan. *See* synagogue of Satan
synagogue of Satan, 10, 80–83, 86–88, 126

Tacitus, 137–38
temple(s). *See* First Temple, Second Temple, 101, 112–17, 122
 pagan. *See also* Pantheon, 118, 137
temptation. *See* tribulation, 66, 72, 88, 91, 116
tēreō, 67, 92
Thyatira, xvi, 3, 13–14, 18, 95, 123
Tiberius, 120
tribulation (trial/testing), 10, 80, 88, 93, 95, 105–8
 of the time of God's judgment in the Tribulation. *See* Tribulation
Tribulation. *See also* Tribulation saints, Great Tribulation, 14, 93, 95, 142
Tribulation saints, 95, 119
Trinity, 22–23, 132
trumpet(s), 22, 91, 99–100
 as associated with the Rapture. *See* Rapture
Turkey, xvi, 139–41
 and taking of Philadelphia, 139–41
types, referring to the seven churches as positive and negative models, 2–5, 18, 92–93, 110

Vespasian, 120
vineyard(s), 15, 89, 136–39

wedding, Jewish, 99–100
witnessing. *See* evangelism, missions, 11, 31, 33, 51, 70, 80
 of Jesus as the true witness, 16, 33–34
Word of God, Jesus as, 92, 103, 109
worldview(s), 6, 31, 51, 85

Yeshua, 73, 77–79, 107

Scripture Index

Old Testament

Genesis

3	37, 39
3:5b	72
3:6	39n2
3:15	39
12:1–7	87
13:14–17	87
15:1b	77
15:6	77

Exodus

3:5b	22
15	28
19	22
19:16b	22
19:18	22
23:2a	87
34:22–23	101

Leviticus

11	24–25
11:3	24
11:4	24
11:6	24
11:7	24
11:9–12	24
11:13–19	24
11:29–30	24
11:44–45	25
19:2b	25
20:7	25
20:7a	26
20:8	25
20:8b	26

Numbers

22–24	12
25:1–3	12
31:16	12

Deuteronomy

4:3	12
32:21b	85

Judges

21:25	16

2 Samuel

7	38, 45
7:13b	38
7:16	39

SCRIPTURE INDEX

1 Kings

5–8	113
7:15–22	113
7:21	114
16:31	13–14
18:4a	13
18:13a	13
21:1–26	13

2 Kings

18–19	40
18	42
18:18	42
18:37	42

2 Chronicles

2–8	113
16:9a	67

Psalms

1	28
2	39n2
14	21
14:1b	21
14:3b	21
16	102
27:4	113
34:9–10	127
34:22	107
89:29b	39
96:9	22
104:33	28
106:28	12
116:15	11
119	53
119:2	127
119:16	127
119:66	127
121:8	55

Proverbs

3:5b	81
16:6a	39n2
18:10	107

Song of Solomon

2:1–2	117
4:13	117
5:13	117
6:2	117
6:11	117
7:12	117

Isaiah

4:2	73
6:4	23
6:5a	23
9:6–7	104
11:1	73
14	74–75
14:13b–14	74
22	40–42, 46–47
22:16	41
22:17–19	41
22:20–22	41
22:20b	42
22:22	47
24:17	93
26:21	93
36–37	40
41:22–23	32
43:6–7	115
44:7–8	31
45:20–21	32
45:21b	21
45:22–23	76
45:22	21
55	124
55:1–3	124
55:3	124
55:6	76
64:4	120

Jeremiah

9	56, 65
9:23–24	56
23:5	73
33	39
33:15	73

SCRIPTURE INDEX

33:17	39
33:20–21	39
33:25–26	39
52:20–23	113

Ezekiel

40–48	87

Daniel

9	93, 96
11	136

Hosea

5:15	84
9:10	12

Joel

2	102

Zechariah

6	73
6:11–13	79
6:12b	73
12	84
14	99

Malachi

3:1a	34
4:5	33

New Testament

Matthew

1:21b	73
2:20	64
3:15	34
3:17	34
5–7	111
5–6	53
5	7, 61
5:2–11	61
5:11–12	94
5:14–16	110
5:17	34
5:18	7
5:48	26
6:25	64
7:24–25	115
10	70–71
10:28	70
10:32–33	71
10:39	64
11:13–14	34
11:27b	42
13:41–42	131
13:49–50	131
16	115
16:16–18	115
16:16	115
16:19	115
17:5	34
19:17	63
24	98, 105
24:3	98
24:21–22	95
24:21b	142
24:30	99
24:37–42	99
24:37–41	105
24:42	97, 106, 127
24:44b	97
25	43
25:13	98, 106, 127
25:21	43
25:23	43
25:41	131
25:46	131
26:53	58
28:18b	115
28:19–20	50

Mark

6:14	34
12	63
12:29–31	63
12:30	65
13	98

153

SCRIPTURE INDEX

Luke

1:31b	73
1:32–33	39
1:46b	64
1:49	64
8	64, 89–90
8:4–15	96
8:14b	90
8:15b	64, 89
8:16	90
12	41
12:16–21	41
12:20	41
12:21	41
15:10	132
16:10	43
17	98
21	98
23:8	34
24:25–27	33

John

1:9	90
1:12	133
1:16	22
1:29b	33
1:42	115
1:50b	34
3:30	65
5	33
5:19	34
5:30	33–34
5:31	33
5:33	33
5:34a	34
5:36–37	34
5:36	34
5:39	35
5:46	35
5:47	36
6:29b	64
7:31b	34
8:18	34
8:32	36
8:36	36
8:42	36
8:44a	82
8:45	36
8:47	36
8:47a	86
9:41b	17
10	46, 122
10:1–16	47
10:9	46
10:18b	58
10:25	35
10:26–27	36
10:28–29	71
10:30	xviii
10:38	34
10:41b	34
14	31, 37, 42, 111
14:6	xvii, 16, 64
14:6b	29, 36
14:7	42
14:9b	42
14:15	62
14:21–23	37
15	78, 128–29
15:1	129, 141
15:2	106, 116
15:3–5	129
15:3	129–30
15:8–12	129
15:10	63
15:12	63
15:15–17	129
15:18–21	108
15:19b–20a	129
16:2	11, 87
16:33	106
16:33b	93
17:3	xviii
18	32, 35–36
18:11b	58
18:36–38	33
18:37b	36
18:38	36
20:29	91

SCRIPTURE INDEX

Acts

1:4	101
2	4, 104
2:16	102
2:25a	102
2:33b	102
4:12	73
8:1–3	61
9:1–30	61
9:22b	102
10	84
14	51
14:22b	106
14:27b	52
17	68
17:2b–3	102
17:11	69
17:11b	68
17:12a	68
26:25b	102
26:27	102
26:28b	103
28:23b	103

Romans

1	71–74, 78
1:20	71
1:21	71
1:25	72
1:28	72
1:32	72
3	21
3:23	21, 132
5:1	83
6:23	132
8:1–2	133
8:19	78
8:21	74
8:22b	78
8:25	90
8:28b	106
8:29b	106
8:37b	106
9–11	84–85, 87
10	77
10:8b	77
10:9	76, 132
10:12	84
10:19b	85
11:1b	85
11:33–36	86
12:2	125
14:11–12	76
15:4	90
15:5b	90
16:25–26	101
16:25b–26a	44

1 Corinthians

1	55
1:25	56
1:29	56
1:31b	65
2:9	120
3:9	118
3:11–15	117
3:16	118
4:1	43–44
4:1b–2	86
4:2	43
7:19	66–67
9:24	66
10:8	12
10:13	106
12:12–13	4
13	61
15:51–53	104
15:51b	97
15:52	100
15:57	133
16:9	52

2 Corinthians

1:20a	16
2:12	52
2:15a	11
3:6	127
4–5	104
4:6–7	44
4:6	109

2 Corinthians (continued)

4:17–18	108
5:7b	91
5:8	104, 131
5:18	67
12	57
12:1–11	61
12:7b	57
12:8	57
12:9–10	57
12:9	106

Galatians

1	61
3:13–29	82
3:27	141
6:8	74

Ephesians

1:13	132
2	28, 84
2:4–7	120
2:8–10	67, 116
2:13–18	141
2:13–17	84
2:14a	67
2:20b	115
3:10b	115
3:12	47
4	122
4:4	4
4:4a	86
4:15	86
4:15a	45
4:29	45
5	4
5:1	42
5:2	43
5:8	43
5:15–21	127
5:21–33	104
5:25b	4
5:29–32	4
6:10b	86
6:17	13

Philippians

1	96
1:23	104, 131
2	45, 76–77
2:7a	58
2:9–11	75
2:11	76
2:17	57
2:22–23	76
3	66, 96, 109
3:13	109
3:14–15a	60
3:14	66
3:14b	109
4:8–9	128
4:8	69
4:13	55

Colossians

1:5b	103
1:13	47
1:16a	16
1:17	16
1:18	5, 16
1:19	23
2:6–7	44
2:9–10	23
3:1–17	53
3:1–3	60
3:4	60
3:14b	60
4:3b	52
4:4b	52

1 Thessalonians

4	96, 98–99, 102, 108
4:16–18	91
4:16–17	104
4:16b	99
4:17	99
4:18	100
5:9	99
5:21b–22	64

SCRIPTURE INDEX

2 Thessalonians

2	96

1 Timothy

4	96
4:1a	94

2 Timothy

2	52
2:12b	71
2:13	71
3:12b	93
3:13b	94
3:16–17	7, 127
4:3–4	94
4:6	57

Titus

2:11–13	91
2:14	127

Hebrews

1:2	142
3:3b	118
3:4	118
4:12	13, 104
6:10	43
9:27	131
10:14b	26
10:23–25	110
10:36	90
11	75, 79
11:6	49, 75–77, 116
11:16	119
12:1–2	130
12:1b	90
12:14	23

James

1:21b–22	103
2:19	77
2:19b	74
4:8	127
5:11a	90
5:11b	90

1 Peter

1	65
1:7b	106
1:13	65
1:15	24
1:16	24
1:22	28
2	52
2:9–10	87
2:22	25
4:10	43
4:12	93
5:6–7	107
5:8–9	107
5:10	106

2 Peter

1:20b	6
1:21	6
2:19	74
3:13–14	111

1 John

1:8	26
1:9	27
2	126
2:2–5	63
2:3–5	126
2:15–17	126
2:18	142
3:2	78
3:23–24	63
3:23	59

Revelation

1	9, 18, 110
1:3	xvii, 1, 8, 100
1:7	99
1:12–13	110

SCRIPTURE INDEX

Revelation *(continued)*

1:18b	47
1:20	110
2–3	xvi, xviii, 1, 5, 7, 9, 18, 87, 92, 110, 112, 123, 135–36, 142
2	3, 18
2:1b	9
2:2b	10
2:4b	10
2:5	10, 110
2:6	10
2:7a	xvii, 1
2:7b	10
2:9	10, 80
2:9b	81
2:10b	11
2:11a	1
2:12–17	135
2:12b	11
2:13a, c	11
2:13b	12
2:14a	12
2:14b	12
2:15	13
2:16	13
2:17	13
2:17a	1
2:18b	13
2:19	13
2:20b	14
2:22	14
2:22b	95
2:23	14
2:24	14
2:27	14
2:29	1
3	xix, xx, 16, 18, 23, 31, 40–41, 46, 60, 81, 93, 95–96, 113, 116, 119, 125, 127, 130–31, 140–42
3:1	14
3:1b	14
3:2b	14
3:3b	15
3:4	15
3:5	15
3:6	1
3:7–8	115
3:7	20, 38, 58, 115
3:7b	46
3:8	62, 67, 70, 89
3:8b	54–55
3:9	80, 89
3:9b	81, 83
3:10	88–92
3:12	112, 120
3:12b	117
3:13	1–2, 123
3:14	16
3:14b	16
3:16b	94
3:17	94
3:17b	17, 94
3:18	17
3:19	95
3:20	17
3:22	1, 17
7	95
8:13	93
11:10	93
12	66
12:17b	66
13	30, 96
13:14	93
17:8	93
19	95, 99
19:12b	121
20:10–15	75
20:11–15	131
21–22	44, 116, 119, 131
21	10
21:3b	119
21:4	120
21:22	116
22	10, 98, 119
22:3–4	119
22:14	120
22:20b	98, 122
22:20c	122

www.ingramcontent.com/pod-product-compliance
Lightning Source LLC
Chambersburg PA
CBHW072134160426
43197CB00012B/2105